Instructor's Resource Manual

D0879648

Instructor's Resource Manual

Kelly S. Mayhew
San Diego City College

to accompany

RACE, CLASS, AND GENDER IN THE UNITED STATES
AN INTEGRATED STUDY

Sixth Edition

Paula S. Rothenberg

WORTH PUBLISHERS

Instructor's Resource Manual
by Kelly S. Mayhew
to accompany
Rothenberg: **Race, Class, and Gender in the United States,** Sixth Edition

Copyright © 2004, 2001 by Worth Publishers

ISBN: 0-7167-5967-5

First Printing

Printed in the United States of America

Worth Publishers
41 Madison Avenue
New York, NY 10010
www.worthpublishers.com

Contents

PART VIII *Making a Difference: Social Activism* *61*

General Introduction

The central argument that students will encounter in Paula Rothenberg's *Race, Class, and Gender in the United States,* sixth edition, is that categories of race, class, gender, and sexuality are socially constructed: they are neither natural, universal, nor inevitable, yet they have real effects on our lives. This means that everyone is subject to social processes. Hence, it is not just women who are gendered but also men. The experiences of heterosexuals, as well as gays and lesbians, are marked by their sexuality. White people, along with people of color, live racially structured lives. And class touches the middle-class, as well as poor and working-class people. In other words, any system of differentiation shapes those on whom it bestows privilege as well as those whom it oppresses. Thus, in a social context in which white people have often viewed themselves as nonracial or racially neutral, it is crucial to look at the "racialness" of white experience. Likewise, in a context in which heterosexuality is viewed as normative (the unacknowledged default position), it is crucial to look at the construction of heterosexuality.

As I have shown in previous editions of this *Instructor's Resource Manual,* the process of thinking through social constructions is a complicated one and is best approached with certain strategies in mind. First, students will be asked to adopt a conscious process in which they think about race, class, and gender categories that they may have taken for granted as "real" or "true" in the sense that they seem permanent, immutable, or at least inevitable and not worth resisting. Second, students should consider their role in maintaining these inequities, whether they are on the side of privilege or not, and to carefully attend to the impact of these categories on themselves, on others, and on society at large. For some students, this process of reflection is already going on in their lives; for others, it will be a process initiated by you, their instructor. Such an initiation can be exciting and dynamic. It can also be painful for students, so it is important to be aware of how fundamentally the materials and frameworks in this text can affect the ways students map out their world. Thus, some students will be moved to question themselves and the social categories of exclusion in which they live, and their questions might lead to political action. Others, however, after thinking through race, class, gender, and sexuality will continue justifying the status quo and rationalizing their place within it. All kinds of students will nevertheless benefit from the exposure to this material, as all of us, teachers as well as students, need to be conscious of the histories and specificities of our cultural positions. The point of teaching material such as this is that it is, itself, part of the solution for social change.

AUDIENCE

As I discovered from the reception of previous editions of this manual, our challenge to appeal to a wide-ranging audience was successful. *Race, Class, and Gender in the United States* tries to account for a student population that extends from elite universities to community colleges, from advanced to basic composition courses, from introductory women's studies courses to upper-division ethnic studies classes, from general education sociology or American pluralism sections to courses for social work majors. I have tried to use the material that worked in the last edition, while adding fresh questions and assignments that not only account for the new essays in the sixth edition but also flesh out some areas that were in the previous manual. The fact that Rothenberg's text is taught in so many kinds of classrooms, to so many kinds of audiences, is testimony to its scope, its significance, and its necessity. I mention this, first, by way of reminding you of the good company you keep and, second, by way of explaining the structure of the assignments that follow.

CHALLENGES FOR STUDENTS AND INSTRUCTORS

The primary emphasis in these assignments is to *stimulate critical thinking, analysis,* and *reflection.* Critical thinking, however, does not occur in a vacuum: the content on which thought processes act has an effect on what knowledge is produced. Thus, I have repeatedly emphasized the specific kinds of thinking that the content of the book encourages. Students will, hopefully, begin to *denaturalize,* through critical and historical investigation, categories that have come to constitute the seemingly natural; *understand,* through analysis, the process by which such mystification occurs; and *reflect* on the effects of racism, sexism, heterosexism, class discrimination, and the like.

The material and the assignments are challenging (i.e., difficult *and* sometimes threatening). Students will have to work through and struggle with some hard concepts to make sense of what is at stake. The text will ask some students to radically revise their understanding of the world and its organization; you should anticipate some resistance from them. Other students will feel that they have nothing to say, as they will recognize their relative privilege and (erroneously) conclude that because they have never "suffered" in the ways the people they read about have, they have nothing concrete to offer the class. You can ask these students to focus on looking at the ways they may be privileged and recognize its epistemological implications: What knowledge have they lost or do they lose *because of* their privilege? For still others, the material will confirm things they have long suspected. Students who find their experiences reflected on the pages of *Race, Class, and Gender in the United States* can gain a vocabulary with which to describe the structure of their lives. In part because of the wide-ranging responses the material will elicit from different student populations, the writing exercises are designed to steer attention away from the students' own reactions to the materials and focus it instead on the structural issues at stake.

THE INTEGRATED APPROACH

The assignments are written as broadly as possible, to be adapted to the needs of your classroom and curriculum. Rothenberg's integrated approach to the theoretical concepts has been maintained at the pedagogical level as well; many of the assignments have been designed to connect with readings in other sections of the book. This has several advantages. First, it reminds students of concepts they have encountered elsewhere in the collection; or, if they haven't yet been exposed to that material, it may prompt them to look at it now. Second, for instructors assigning selective sections and sections in non-chronological order, this approach points out connections to useful pieces students may otherwise miss. The third, and perhaps most important advantage of this integrated approach, is that it encourages students to explore the book on their own, to find pieces that speak to them. In my experience, this is one of the most useful aspects of teaching the book. In this process of discovery, even the most resistant students come to "own" certain writings that they'll recall long after the semester has passed. I highly recommend allowing or even assigning students to wander through the book at some point in the term.

TYPES OF ASSIGNMENTS

The format of the assignments in this manual roughly conforms to the idea generation-writing-research model of college classroom writing. I kept to this general format so that instructors in a wide variety of fields and disciplines would be able to readily adapt assignments to their needs. This three-part writing structure is highly flexible and has the advantage of not necessarily leading to a piece of writing as the finished product. For example, the

Generating Ideas/Small-Group Discussions exercises can also be the basis of preparation for exams, and instructors can vary the assignments as needed for their specific disciplines. In addition, the assignment portion of this text is directed at the student, so you may reproduce assignments directly from the manual and distribute them if you choose.

The parts in the manual correspond with the parts of Rothenberg's book. Within each part, there are *Issues and Questions to Consider* that the instructor can use as the basis for freewriting exercises or classroom discussion; a *Generating Ideas/Small-Group Discussion* section that helps students begin the critical thinking, reading, and writing processes; *Writing Assignments* that focus on writing single essays; *Research/Analysis Projects,* some of which make connections to materials elsewhere in the collection and some that require outside research; and, finally, a *Recommended Media* section that provides some suggestions for films, documentaries, music, Internet sites, TV shows, and so on, that can accompany and expand your use of the book. The idea-generating exercises can be used as the basis for classroom discussion or journal writing exercises. Several questions in each section ask students to draw connections between pieces. As I mentioned earlier, instructors who don't assign the entire book can still have students use materials from other areas. This approach also encourages students to draw on their own interests to explore the book.

ENCOURAGING CRITICAL THINKING

The primary focus in this manual has been on encouraging critical thinking, so in the assignments there is less attention on the self-expressive component many first-year students rely on (though I haven't entirely eliminated that type of assignment). This strategy is both theoretical and pedagogical. Some students (in any classroom) feel threatened by writing exercises that ask them to examine or reveal themselves, or their feelings about and reactions to the material. In the case of the essays in the text, that feeling can be exacerbated by the sensitivity of the subject matter. The risk is that students will reject everything that you're attempting to convey to them. Focusing on the structural aspects of the issues at hand rather than on personal reactions to those issues can alleviate some of this resistance. For this reason, you might downplay the expressive writing assignments but leave students room to figure out their place within the social scheme.

USING MEDIA IN THE CLASSROOM

I chose to include a *Recommended Media* section in each part of the manual because I believe that students will benefit from actually *seeing* how the issues *Race, Class, and Gender in the United States* raises are represented. While by no means comprehensive, I've taken great care in choosing various types of media my colleagues or I have used or would want to use in our own classes. It is important to supplement Rothenberg's text with interdisciplinary materials. The media that have been chosen cover a range from documentaries, "serious" films, and popular movies to photographs, folk music, and Internet sites. The listings are meant as suggestions only, and some of them require that you do research in order to find the media sources in your area. You might also consider assigning a novel or other supplementary text, or sending your students to museums or cultural events. When students experientially explore the concepts from the textbook, their writing will improve, as they will have more to write about and will feel even more engaged with the ideas in Rothenberg's text.

FINAL THOUGHTS

This manual is different from others because it does not have assignments to accompany every article in the book. Rather, each set of assignments has been designed to stimulate your own thinking and teaching and to encourage the flexible use of this text.

There is another important difference to this text: it is my position that all texts (be they advertisements, essays, poems, films, or narrative fiction) convey *arguments*. The worldviews presented in materials that seem lacking in arguments are precisely those that can be most insidious because they are purportedly neutral. I highly recommend that you review and assign Rothenberg's introductory essays to each part in the book and the "Further Reading" selections at the end of each chapter. The introductions provide excellent overviews of the material, and the bibliographies give students a place to start for research projects or for their own continuing studies.

A Note to Community College Instructors

Race, Class, and Gender in the United States lends itself very well to the community college setting. With Rothenberg's emphasis on analysis of systemic issues and her illumination of the ways we are all socially constructed by the society in which we live, students in community college classrooms will find a great deal in the text that speaks to their own experiences in life. While some might have trouble engaging with the essays' confrontation of social, cultural, and historical issues, many more will probably find that the material provides them with important tools for thinking about their own particular social contexts. The foregrounding of issues of economics and class, particularly, will speak to students in community colleges. Whether they are Latino, Latin American, African, African American, Asian, Indian, Jewish, European American, Eastern European, Native American, white, black, brown, yellow, or red, students from all ethnicities and/or races will often find that they share certain affinities with regard to economic class. As so many students attend community colleges because of economic hardship, discussions of how their lives have been informed by such issues can be particularly fruitful in such a setting.

The textbook's collection of essays concerning *difference* and its construction will also speak to the diverse population a community college often serves. Students will respond to how the essays explore, rather than demonize, the manner in which race, class, gender, and sexuality are constructed in the United States. Often, they themselves, because of their own class background, ethnicity, race, gender, or sexuality (or combinations of these categories), have felt marginalized or left out of society. Many students attend community colleges in order to improve their lives and to acquire an education or skills that will enable them to either transfer to a four-year university or get a better job. A text such as *Race, Class, and Gender in the United States* can be useful for such students by helping them see that their particular place in American society is not a natural, inevitable phenomenon, but rather a product of social and historical forces, and is thus changeable. For students to realize that attitudes, ideas, and constructions of various modes of thinking are fluid and products of historical processes can be enormously empowering—especially for people who might need support to continue on in their education and their new paths in life.

6

Such sensitivity to the struggles students are engaged in can make for a lively classroom and heated discussion. When students feel included, when texts speak to their experience of the world and give them tools or language to describe their place in society, they are actively engaged and bound to benefit from exposure to new ways of thinking. As I mentioned in the general introduction, students must also confront, rather than discount, concepts in this text that might make them uncomfortable. They need to learn how to think their way through difficult issues instead of merely dismissing them as "politically correct" or ignoring them altogether. This is why the assignments in this manual focus so much on facilitating critical thinking.

SPECIFIC BENEFITS TO THE COMMUNITY COLLEGE STUDENT

The assignments in the manual can be particularly useful in a community college writing classroom, as a great deal of discussion often goes into defining and exploring terms, ideas, and ways of looking at issues. Another aspect of this manual that will be useful for community college instructors is the emphasis on group work, small-group discussions, idea-generating assignments, and journal writing. The assignments provide ample space for exploration and definition of terms in order to give students the time they might need to really think through their perspectives and their ideas before beginning the writing process. Indeed, this manual is designed to encourage students to see the writing process as a continuum: from critical reading and thinking to crafting an essay. Much as Rothenberg sees the essays in the text as engaging in non-oppositional thinking about issues of race, class, gender, and sexuality, this manual does the same sort of thing for class assignments. The process orientation of the manual lends itself well to the sort of teaching that happens in a community college classroom where a great deal of work goes into helping students see reading and writing as useful and beneficial skills, and not as torturous, impossible tasks. By emphasizing process and idea formation, I hope to help community college instructors use *Race, Class, and Gender in the United States* in their classrooms in the most effective ways possible.

LEVEL OF LANGUAGE

Finally, a word about the language in the essays. This text contains a variety of voices, some very colloquial and others fairly theoretically sophisticated. As Rothenberg notes in *Race, Class, and Gender in the United States,* she deliberately chose readings that would speak to various reading levels. Many students may have trouble negotiating the language in the more difficult essays. In the manual, therefore, I have tried to focus students' attention on key terms in order to allow them to define such ideas for themselves. By drawing students' attention to the words that might give them the most trouble, the power of definition is placed squarely in their court. While some essays might not be appropriate for all levels of community college classes, instructors should feel confident that with a little extra work, the ideas for thinking and writing that the essays contain will lead to wonderfully complex and interesting learning and essay writing. Thus, for any community college course that contains either a critical thinking or research component, Rothenberg's text offers challenging, useful, and important material to aid in such endeavors.

PART I

The Social Construction of Difference: Race, Class, Gender, and Sexuality

Part I delineates some of the many ways society forms human subjects and their attitudes toward themselves and others, as well as the ways differences between and among people are created and maintained. Through her selection of pieces, Rothenberg wants to draw attention to how differences occur and how hierarchies are established from such perceived differences. Beginning with discussions of race and ethnicity, Rothenberg then covers gender, sexuality, and class in her effort to denaturalize the very aspects of ourselves that we take to be the most "natural." Thus, the essays dealing with sexuality, for example, are often very interesting to students because they make them look at the ways the most personal parts of themselves are subject to social construction.

ISSUES AND QUESTIONS TO CONSIDER

(The topics that appear under *Issues and Questions to Consider* in each part are designed to help you initiate class discussions and clarify aspects of the readings that might be confusing or challenging for your students.)

- Part I establishes the themes that will be repeated throughout the volume. This is the time to emphasize to students the economic and historical basis for socially constructed categories. Race categories are born of economic conflict. Gender categories, likewise, function economically. When economics shift, so do these categories.

- Emphasize to your students the idea that social constructs are real—as evidenced by many of the essays in this section—in that they have effects. This is different, however, from saying that they are natural or inevitable. They are constructed, and there is historical evidence to

9

prove it. As Judith Lorber says in "'Night to His Day': The Social Construction of Gender," "Whatever genes, hormones, and biological evolution contribute to human social institutions is materially as well as qualitatively transformed by social practices. Every social institution has a material base, but culture and social practices transform that base into something with qualitatively different patterns and constraints." You might discuss what she means by this.

- Many students want to see differences as necessary and useful defining characteristics of human beings. To discuss issues of race and ethnicity, gender, sexuality, and class as social constructs, with no inherently "natural" meanings, is often unsettling to students who may desperately want to emphasize differences between men and women or between other groups. Students often feel that if differences are discussed and evaluated in class, they are being asked to eliminate them altogether—an impossibility in our current society. But as a point of departure for discussion, take a topic from Part I, such as race, and talk about what society would be like if no racial differences existed. What would such a society look like? Such an exercise is useful for making distinctions between the idea that no differences should exist and the idea that differences in this culture represent the ways various people are defined hierarchically depending on the color of their skin, their ethnic background, their gender, their sexuality, or their class. In other words, differences do exist, and the point is not necessarily that there shouldn't, for example, be any distinctions between men and women; but rather that the ways each gender is *valued* in this culture can be extremely unfair and even dangerous. A useful way to end this discussion would be to bring in Jean Baker Miller's piece, "Domination and Subordination." Who is dominant? Who is subordinate? Why?

- In "The Ethics of Living Jim Crow," Richard Wright describes what it was like to grow up under laws and attitudes that assumed black people and white people were two different species, with whites being inherently more valuable than blacks. Although the laws were overturned during the civil rights struggles of the fifties and sixties, attitudes and ideologies are harder to deal with. Drawing on the work of Michael Omi, Howard Winant, and Pem Davidson Buck, how have things changed? How are they the same? How does the history of slavery and Jim Crow affect the ways African American identities are socially constructed in our contemporary society? To what end?

- Ask students to consider questions of history. In current debates, recent immigrants—especially "illegal" ones—have been demonized by everyone from politicians and the mass media to people who have benefited from their labor. Karen Brodkin's piece provides an overview of the history and immigration patterns of Jews in America, and it offers a perspective on recent discussions of the "problems" of immigration. How do students view this history? How does it affect their understanding of contemporary approaches to immigration? What do they make of the fact that "white" groups were discriminated against in the past as "others"? How does an understanding of history facilitate one's analysis of current issues or problems?

- What are the multiple ways gender is socially constructed? What are the stereotypes surrounding femininity? Masculinity? What happens when someone does not fit these norms? What is the difference between "sex" and "gender" (Lorber, Hubbard, Kimmel)?

- What happens to one's view of sexuality when one does not see it as "natural"? How does that influence or change attitudes toward homosexuality or bisexuality, for example? If heterosexuality is a social construct, what about procreation? What role does biology play in the construction and maintenance of sexuality? What happens when one disconnects sexuality from gender? When one stops seeing men as inherently sexual and women as asexual or merely as sexualized objects (Hubbard, Katz, Kimmel)?

- What happens to one's view of "disability" when one stops defining it as a "condition," but rather sees it also as being socially constructed? How has the language of disability permeated our culture to such an extent that it is used consciously and unconsciously to dismiss or denigrate the contributions of various constituencies in U.S. society? In what way does such language encourage or facilitate inequality, as Douglas Baynton puts it in his piece? And how does such language discount disabled people?

- In "Deconstructing the Underclass," Herbert Gans discusses how the public's perception of class is shaped by the terms we use to describe it. How are poor or working-class people viewed in this society? How does the concept of nature tie into who belongs in what class? What are the pitfalls of thinking about this country as being either "classless" or as having a huge middle class to which everyone belongs?

ASSIGNMENTS

Generating Ideas/Small-Group Discussions

ASSIGNMENT 1. In almost all of the essays in Part I, race, gender, sexuality, and class are analyzed as, to use Omi and Winant's term, "pre-eminently *sociohistorical* concept[s]" (I, 1). That is, things "are given concrete expression by the specific social relations and historical context in which they are embedded." In your journal, take a page to discuss an aspect of race, gender, sexuality, or class as a "sociohistorical concept." How is your view of race or ethnicity different from the views held by people during the period Richard Wright describes in his piece "The Ethics of Living Jim Crow" (I, 2)? How are gender relations different now than in your parents' time? How does the current configuration of the government affect the way class is talked about? When you consider answers to these questions, avoid thinking in terms of "progress"—that is, that "things are better now than in the past." The point of addressing these questions in your journal is to get you to think about social relations as inherently complicated *processes* that certainly change over time, but don't always change for the better.

ASSIGNMENT 2. At the beginning of "Racial Formations" (I, 1), Omi and Winant describe the case of Susie Guillory Phipps, who tried to sue the Louisiana Bureau of Vital Records in order "to change her racial classification from black to white." As the authors point out, this case brings to the fore questions concerning the definition of race and how people are racially marked. In a small group, discuss the ways each group member is "marked" racially. What, for example, is your whiteness composed of, if that is how you define yourself? Your blackness? Your brownness? How is ethnicity "marked" in this culture? What are the implications of such marking for society? After you have spent several minutes on this task, spend a few more writing a page discussing what you learned about yourself and others. Evaluate yourself as a "raced" person. How do you fit into a culture that insists on marking its members?

ASSIGNMENT 3. Karen Brodkin (I, 4) describes her "surprise" that immigrant workers, such as Jews, were not always considered "white," since she grew up in a community that did not mark her as "ethnic." What do you make of her generational discussion of the ways immigrants became "white"? What does this essay say about whiteness? About the racialization of immigration? Why are contemporary immigrants seen as "dark," when many, in fact, are "white"?

ASSIGNMENT 4. On the chalkboard, your instructor will write down four categories: FEMALE/MALE, WOMAN/MAN. These are meant to make a distinction between categories of "sex" and "gender." Spend several minutes as a class listing the stereotypes or attributes of these beings under each category. What can you come up with? What do these stereotypes show about the ways people view sex and gender? Are these categories set in stone? How are various attributes valued or devalued in our society? Why are they valued and devalued? Also think about how quickly you were able to come up with these stereotypes. What do you think this says about the staying power of stereotypes in this society?

You can also do a similar exercise with class and ability: Divide the board up into four categories, POOR/WORKING CLASS/MIDDLE CLASS/UPPER CLASS, or into two categories, ABLED/DISABLED. How are these categories valued or devalued in this culture? What attributes are assigned to people in these categories? How did these attributes come into being, do you think?

ASSIGNMENT 5. In "The Invention of Heterosexuality" (I, 7), Jonathan Ned Katz not only highlights the ways heterosexuality is socially constructed but also historicizes the process by which such construction occurs. You may be challenged by Katz's assertion that one is not born but made heterosexual, which should lead to both lively discussions and interesting writing. After discussing the essay in class—and perhaps pairing it with Lorber's piece (I, 5), Hubbard's "The Social Construction of Sexuality" (I, 6), and Kimmel's "Masculinity as Homophobia" (I, 8)— write a one- to two-page response/critique of Katz's article in your journal or as a homework assignment. What new ideas did you learn from the essay? Have you ever thought that something like sexuality could be socially constructed? In your own life, how have you noticed sexuality or gender as being constructed? How does homophobia function to regulate so-called "normal" sexual and gender identities? As a class, spend a week documenting ways that gender and sexuality are constructed. At the end of the week, reconvene and discuss everyone's findings as a class.

Writing Assignments

ASSIGNMENT 6. Read Jean Baker Miller's "Domination and Subordination" (I, 11) and consider the questions she poses at the beginning of the piece:

> When does the engagement of difference stimulate the development and the enhancement of both parties to the engagement? And, conversely, when does such a confrontation with difference have negative effects: When does it lead to great difficulty, deterioration, and distortion and to some of the worst forms of degradation, terror, and violence—both for individuals and for groups—that human beings can experience?

Pick two hypothetical instances of what she describes and discuss them. When does one learn from encountering difference? When does such an encounter lead to difficulty? Try to keep your essay focused on the institutional or systemic. You might look at issues surrounding bilingual education in schools, the history of mandatory or voluntary busing, women in the work-place, or the living-wage movement (where a livable income would replace the minimum wage).

ASSIGNMENT 7. Read "Racial Formations" (I, 1) and "The Ethics of Living Jim Crow" (I, 2), "Constructing Race, Creating White Privilege" (I, 3), and/or "How Jews Became White Folks" (I, 4). How do Wright's, Buck's, and Brodkin's pieces illustrate what Omi and Winant are writing about? Focus your essay on two or three aspects where each piece echoes the other. For example, how does Wright describe his early process of "racialization" (Omi and Winant) as a boy living in Arkansas? How does Buck integrate discussions of laws regarding race and "race mixing" into her analysis of the construction of whiteness? What does Brodkin say about the linkage of whiteness and middle class-ness? How does Wright describe his racial consciousness as a "sociohistorical concept" (Omi and Winant)? Instead of the Wright, Buck, or Brodkin pieces, you can also use an article from Part V and talk about how people from other ethnic groups undergo similar racializing processes.

ASSIGNMENT 8. Read Judith Lorber's "'Night to His Day': The Social Construction of Gender" (I, 5). Take a moment to think about the clothes you are wearing and the ways you dress yourself. How does Lorber's piece help you analyze the ways you construct yourself? How do clothing fash-ions aid in the social construction of gender? What does a woman or man say about herself or himself with various pieces of clothing? Write an essay in which you explore these issues.

Research/Analysis Projects

ASSIGNMENT 9. From your journal or homework assignments on Katz's "The Invention of Heterosexuality" (I, 7), look at a particular practice or phenomenon (homosexuality, heterosexuality, bisexuality, gendered fashions, particular words—"straight," "queer"—or phrases, behaviors, etc.) and formulate a thesis statement or argument about it. How is this practice or phenomenon viewed by society? Why? What effect does this point of view have on the people who live their lives in this way? An interesting research project might be for you to look at a history of sexuality in America and examine a practice in a historical and contextual frame. If you are heterosexual, how did you come to act the way you do? What in the culture (films, ads, TV shows, books, Valentine's Day, etc.) presents a model for your way of being? In other words, place a contemporary sexual role or gendered behavior in the past in context, and talk about how the past construction impacts contemporary constructions of your topic.

ASSIGNMENT 10. Omi and Winant primarily discuss the social construction of African Americans as black, and what that construction has meant historically as well as currently. Take another group—Latinos, Asians, or Native Americans, for instance—and do a similar analysis. Research the group's history in the United States. What were early constructions of this group's racial/ethnic attributes? How have people from several countries or regions been collapsed into one general category (e.g. "Asians," which stands in for people who are from a wide range of places such as China, Japan, Korea, Thailand, India, and Pakistan)? How does this impact the way these people are viewed by the dominant society? How does this lumping erase essential differences between people's distinct cultures? What have these groups become in contemporary parlance? How are they constructed in everyday life by the media, the government, and schools? Brodkin's "How Jews Became White Folks" (I, 4) and Buck's "Constructing Race, Creating White Privilege" (I, 3) are useful essays to draw from here.

ASSIGNMENT 11. While reading Lorber's article (I, 5), pay close attention to her discussion of sports. You might also look at Kimmel's piece in this part (I, 8), and Sabo's and Jordan's pieces in Part V. With the fairly recent addition of the Women's National Basketball Association to the summer sports lineup and the success of women's soccer teams, how do male and female athletes compare? How are they constructed in the media? To do this project, you might survey several issues of sports magazines, such as *Sports Illustrated,* and watch several days of ESPN, Fox Sports, and other sports programming. What do these mass-mediated outlets do in their constructions of femininity and masculinity? Of sexuality? Of race and ethnicity?

ASSIGNMENT 12. After reading Gans's article, "Deconstructing the Underclass" (I, 10) research and discuss how poor people are portrayed in contemporary culture. You might want to refer to the two articles by Gregory Mantsios (Parts II and VII), in particular, "Media Magic: Making Class Invisible" (VII, 112). Survey the news media or popular culture for ways that the poor are represented. How do such portrayals affect people's vision of the poor and of themselves? Are there any mass-media representations that do not fall into easy stereotyping? If so, what are they and how are their representations different from the norm? You might compare and contrast a couple of different constructions of the poor or working classes to illustrate your arguments.

ASSIGNMENT 13. After reading "Domination and Subordination" by Jean Baker Miller (I, 11), write an essay in which you analyze the concept of the "dominant group." You might also refer to Buck's (I, 3) and Brodkin's (I, 4) essays on whiteness, Katz's essay on heterosexuality (I, 7), Kimmel's piece on masculinity (I, 8), Gans's article on class (I, 10), and perhaps incorporate some of Baynton's observations about the language of ability and disability (I, 9). How does dominance operate in U.S. society? What happens when you make visible the dominant groups? Is it important to understand this concept? Why or why not? What can we gain from understanding how such dominance is constructed and maintained? Make sure to provide specific examples to illustrate your points.

RECOMMENDED MEDIA

- Show Spike Lee's *Do the Right Thing*. What is "doing the right thing" for Lee's character? What do the race relations in this film show about the ways people construct each other through the lens of skin color? How do issues of class play out in the film? In other words, why does Lee's character keep working in the pizza parlor, even though he is treated as less than human at times?

- Show *American History X* and discuss how the film deals with the making of a racist and the unmaking of one. Does the film work? Why or why not? What roles do class and masculinity play in the film?

- To interrogate issues of the "naturalness" of gender or sexuality, show *Paris is Burning* or *Wigstock*. How do these films foreground the constructedness of gender roles and sexuality? How do they contest the "naturalness" of femininity as attached to women and masculinity as attached to men?

- Show the "Malibu Stacey" episode of *The Simpsons*. Why does Lisa want to make her own talking Barbie-like doll? What does this episode say about how dolls contribute to gender role construction? With the class, you might also interrogate Grandpa Simpson's own journey. What is this episode doing with age and ageism?

- Show the film *My Left Foot*. Even though this film is set in Britain, how does the story of Christy Brown's life and how he dealt with his cerebral palsy illustrate Baynton's points about disability and the language of disability? The film reviews all laud Brown's "courage" and "determination" in dealing with his disability, yet he was also hard drinking and had an extremely earthy approach to life. How is our society's penchant for defining disability as "lack" borne out in these reviews? How does this film challenge or uphold our definitions of disability?

PART II

Understanding Racism, Sexism, Heterosexism, and Class Privilege

The essays in Part I examine the concept of social construction and how it can help us see the ways systems of race, class, gender, and sexuality function to establish the boundaries of our lives. Rothenberg's selections in Part II extend our understanding of how racism, sexism, heterosexism, and class privilege operate in extending power to some in this society but not to everyone. Part II also maps out interconnections between the various systems in order to help students comprehend that these "isms" most often work together, overlap, and compound one another. The power of words, of definitions, of language itself is explored in this part's selections, and the essays invite students to consider the multiple ways they might participate in or be impacted by structures of domination. Rothenberg's selection of pieces foregrounds a structural analysis of power relations, and in her introduction she is careful to provide precise definitions for words such as "racism" and "sexism." The pieces here echo Rothenberg's concerns over the sense of these terms. While some students might balk at what they could see as the essays' too-narrow definition of "racism," "sexism," "prejudice," "discrimination," and so on, such resistance should lead to lively conversations regarding the meaning and use of politically charged words. Thus, students will benefit from the authors' careful discussion of how they see racism, sexism, discrimination, prejudice, and privileges of all sorts operating in a range of situations.

ISSUES AND QUESTIONS TO CONSIDER

- Before discussing the essays in this section, ask students for their definitions of the term "political correctness." You may be surprised at some of the answers you get. You then might devote a moment to outlining the history of this term (that it started in left-leaning circles in

17

the sixties to chide someone for being too dogmatic, and that it was picked up by the right in the eighties and nineties to put the brakes on "overly sensitive" speech which, as pundits and politicians saw it, was a result of multicultural education run amok). What are the implications of this term? Can one ever be "too" politically correct? Why or why not? Why might we want to be careful about the way we say or define things?

- Spend time considering the different definitions of "racism" this part explores. Rothenberg, Tatum, Sethi, Tilove, and Marable all discuss this term, and all have somewhat different understandings of the word. Which definition seems to be the most accurate? Why?

- Both Marable and Johnson are male writers considering the concepts of sexism and patriarchy. Discuss with students what they think of men writing about sexism, white people writing about white privilege and racism, heterosexuals writing about homophobia and heterosexism, and middle-class people writing about the poor. In Part VIII, Ayvazian analyzes the concept of "allies." How do some of the authors in Part II model such a concept?

- Spend some time discussing Frye's image of the birdcage. Why is this a useful image for describing oppression? How might you use the image to describe other issues such as racism or class discrimination? Many students have trouble with Frye's door opening discussion. They might believe she "makes too big a deal out of it," that "men are just being nice," and that "I [i.e., women] do it, too—is that bad?" You will probably have to outline how this is an example of a bar in the birdcage very specifically for them.

- In Part I we discussed the social construction of race, gender, sexuality, and class, and the ways these subject positions are designed so that different attributes have differing values. In this part, we are looking at the ways attributes such as race, gender, sexuality, and class are valued negatively, and we are learning how to describe them in order to contest such negative evaluations. Explore with students how such negative evaluations might have come into being. This would be an ideal place to bring in Dovidio and Gaertner's essay, "On the Nature of Contemporary Prejudice," to outline how prejudice operates psychologically. You might also discuss why systems of domination must be religiously policed. Why, for example, if dominant groups so firmly hold power, does there need to be a system of language that enforces the oppression of others? Could it be that dominant groups are not "naturally" better than others but are so by virtue of their skin color, their gender, their sexuality, and/or their class position? In other words, must a system of domination uphold itself in order to distract people from its social construction? Also look at Tatum's or Pharr's pieces to explore these issues.

- Some of the essays discuss internalized racism, sexism, or class privilege. How does this happen? What is the result of such thinking? What solutions might there be to combating this?

- Sethi's and Tilove's articles detail conflicts among "ethnic" populations. Both authors explore the manner in which various groups discriminate against each other, and both authors also try to expand discussions of race and ethnicity beyond a black–white paradigm. How do these discussions help students visualize a more complex society? How might the complication of these issues help students analyze the operation of structures of domination? In particular, regarding prejudices among various people that can be traced to media representations (for instance, of Koreans toward African Americans), how might such sentiments defamiliarize, or make unfamiliar, the very act of stereotyping that occurs daily in this country?

- Many white students might feel uncomfortable with McIntosh's discussion of white privilege. Explore with the class what it means to make whiteness "visible" as a racial category in order to analyze it. How is whiteness rendered "invisible" through ideology, and to what effect?

ASSIGNMENTS

Generating Ideas/Small-Group Discussions

ASSIGNMENT 1. Your instructor will split the class into small groups of about four to five people and then write some terms and "isms" (discrimination, prejudice, ideology, racism, sexism, homophobia, heterosexism, classism or class privilege, ableism, ageism, etc.) on the board. After being assigned a term or "ism," each group should define its assigned concept and come up with a specific example of how the concept operates in everyday life. Each group should then present its findings to the rest of the class in order to begin a discussion of the particular concept.

ASSIGNMENT 2. In Peggy McIntosh's "White Privilege: Unpacking the Invisible Knapsack" (II, 20), readers are confronted by the ways whiteness is made to seem "normal" in the United States. Often it has never occurred to many so-called white people how they can be privileged by virtue of their skin color—even though whiteness is always visible to non-white people. In

a group or individually, identify some way in which you're "privileged"—
that is, by class, by gender, by education, by being part of a tightly knit
community, or in some other way. How does this privilege manifest itself?
Have you ever thought you were privileged in this way? What are your
assumptions about others who do not share this privilege? Discuss your
explorations with the rest of the class.

ASSIGNMENT 3. In your journal, discuss the connections you can make
between Marilyn Frye's birdcage (II, 18) and Beverley Daniels Tatum's discussion of "internalized oppression" (II, 12). What do these two ideas have
in common? How does the birdcage illustrate Tatum's point about members of oppressed groups often "believing the distorted messages about
one's own group"? What specific examples can you come up with that
describe the bars of the cage?

ASSIGNMENT 4. Read the essay by Pharr (II, 19), who argues that homophobia is a debilitating aspect of the culture that affects us all. Did Pharr's
essay make you uncomfortable, or did you find yourself agreeing with her
position? In your journal, describe your reactions to this essay. Isolate specific moments in the piece that troubled you. What portions of the essay
did you admire? In class, discuss this essay and link it up with Marable's
(II, 16), Johnson's (II, 17), and Frye's (II, 18) pieces. How do homophobia
and sexism work as mechanisms of social control?

ASSIGNMENT 5. Spend some time in a small group discussing class.
Before group members share their personal class histories, they should
review Mantsios's "Class in America: Myths and Realities—2003" (II, 21)
in order to clarify their terminology. Individually, members should identify
where they stand with regard to class and why they've chosen to position
themselves there. Finally, they should ask themselves why it's important to
understand one's class position. How does this help you understand class
in America and class discrimination?

ASSIGNMENT 6. In a pair, follow Gregory Mantsios's (II, 21) model of a
hypothetical person, construct identities for yourselves, and interview each
other. (What is your class, race, gender, educational background, and so
on?) After constructing your persons, make some predictions among yourselves about their futures. Will each be a "success"? Why or why not? How
does Mantsios's outlining of the myths and realities of class help you see
what goes into determining a person's future?

ASSIGNMENT 7. After reading Dovidio and Gaertner's article, "On the Nature of Contemporary Prejudice" (II, 13), think about a time you might have expressed some prejudice and write about it in your journal. Did you express this bias overtly? How? How did you feel about it at the time? Later? Write one to two pages on this experience.

Writing Assignments

ASSIGNMENT 8. Take one of the key terms from Part II—racism, sexism, heterosexism, homophobia, oppression, discrimination, prejudice, class discrimination, and so on—and analyze it. If your class has done the "isms" exercise, you might choose a term that your group did *not* investigate, or you might extend your group's findings. Use at least two articles from this part that deal with the term in some way. You might choose to address Rothenberg's concerns in her introduction to Part II in your paper. Do you think a more precise definition of your term is necessary? Or do you think it should be broadened? How do you see your term operating in society? Feel free to draw on a personal narrative from Part V to show how you see your term operating in American society. How would you alter how people are socially constructed in order to eliminate your term? What solutions can you offer to see this happen?

ASSIGNMENT 9. Read a real-life news story from Part III or a personal narrative from another part (Wu, Alsultany, Cofer, Wright, or Terkel would all be good) in order to look at the ways McIntosh's observations about privilege or lack of privilege play out in someone's life (II, 20). What have you learned from looking at things from this perspective? How do you view your own life, your own experiences? What personal experiences have you had that make you think about race and/or ethnicity? About whiteness? Make sure, however, that you tie your own experience into larger, systemic issues. You might also draw on the report by the U.S. Commission on Civil Rights in order to structure your essay (III, 22).

ASSIGNMENT 10. Discuss a birdcage you inhabit or might inhabit (II, 18). What makes up its bars? What structures in society close you in, keep you from having access to the best life you could lead? Or, instead, create a narrative about someone else's birdcage. Try to put yourself in someone else's shoes for a moment and describe what sorts of bars keep him or her in place. Construct someone who is totally different from you, but make sure that you pay attention and are sensitive to the multiple ways the person's life may diverge from your own. What is his or her ethnicity or race?

Gender? Class standing? Occupation? Educational level? Does she or he live in a rural area or an urban one? Is the person in a relationship? What is his or her sexual orientation, and so on? All of these things will affect your construction of that person's or your own birdcage.

Research/Analysis Projects

ASSIGNMENT 11. Read Rita Chaudhry Sethi's essay "Smells Like Racism" (II, 14) carefully and write an essay on a particular ethnic group. How has this group been stereotyped in American society? Why, do you think? How has it been constructed as "other"? In your essay, be sure to research your group so that you can discuss how certain practices are misunderstood by other people in the dominant culture. What is the history of your group in America? What sorts of examples can you come up with about the ways this group has been dealt with in popular culture and in the culture at large? How do other minority and/or immigrant groups perceive this group? Why is this so, do you think? You might go to the U.S. Census website (www.census.gov) and look at some statistics of your group. At any rate, use several sources so that you can do as thorough a job as possible.

ASSIGNMENT 12. Research the relationship between two ethnic groups in this country. Make sure you look at Sethi's (II, 14) and Tilove's (II, 15) articles in this part to help you do this. What is the relationship between your two groups? What is their history with each other? How have cultural stereotypes of each group affected the ways they deal with each other? How can people begin to overcome dangerous and unhealthy stereotypes of each other? How can new constructions of various groups and various people be instituted in this society?

ASSIGNMENT 13. Research some of the articles on "aversive racism." What do the studies show about this phenomenon? How does it operate in our society? Make sure you provide specific examples as well as ample documentation for your discussion.

ASSIGNMENT 14. Research the history behind a gendered behavior as Frye does with door opening (II, 18). Where does this behavior come from? What does it say about the construction of women and men? Can such behaviors ever just be "being nice"? Why or why not?

ASSIGNMENT 15. Research and then write an essay in which you discuss the ownership and control of the media, with a specific focus on race and/or gender issues. Review Marable's (II, 16) and Johnson's (II, 17) articles in which they discuss the impact stereotypes promulgated by the mass media, as controlled largely by whites and men, have had on people of color and women. What are the implications of our mass media's being operated with a narrow definition of what constitutes "normal"? *Who* is "normal" in the mediated world? And who isn't? Who gets stereotyped? And who doesn't? Why is this important to examine and understand? You might also consider Dovidio and Gaertner's points about "aversive racism" (II, 13) and where the negative feelings many whites possess towards people of color might originate from. Can media representations influence how people view each other at a basic level?

RECOMMENDED MEDIA

- Show *Thelma and Louise,* and discuss it in relation to Frye's birdcage. What are Thelma and Louise running away from? Why do they choose death rather than "going back"? What would they be "going back" to? You might also ask your class how their whiteness and heterosexuality combine with their gender. Would this film be different if it were two women of color or two lesbians on the lam from the police and the patriarchal state?

- You might show either *Falling Down* or *Blue Collar* to address issues of white middle-class or white working-class masculinity and oppressive economic structures. *Falling Down* also illustrates some of the points Rita Sethi makes in her article about the film and its representation of "otherness."

- Show John Singleton's film, *Rosewood.* How does it illustrate all levels of discrimination? How does it demonstrate that the term "discrimination" is often not strong enough and cannot stand in for "racism," for instance? What does Singleton's use of history add in drawing out these issues?

- Show the documentary *Hoop Dreams* and discuss the ways the film deals with the intersections of race and class.

Discrimination
in Everyday Life

Part III, composed as it is of recent articles taken directly out of newspapers, magazines, and web sources, attempts to address students' desire to dismiss issues of race, class, gender, and sexuality as problems of the past. After grappling with complex terms and coming to some understanding of how ideology operates in American society, many students feel overwhelmed. The essays in Part III ground the previous explorations of oppression, prejudice, discrimination, and so on, in real-life terms. When students read about a group of women workers being discriminated against in their jobs at Wal-Mart or a gay football player who is unable to come out about his sexuality for fear he will be kicked off his team, issues of sexism, homophobia, and the like, are made concrete. Students are then able to go on and discover for themselves how such inequalities are a day-to-day reality for many people in this society. Part III also provides a fine introduction to the personal narratives of Part V. For courses that have a research component, this section gives students a great deal of material that they can use as examples in their own work. Part III also provides a wide range of sources that students can use to support their arguments in their writing projects.

ISSUES AND QUESTIONS TO CONSIDER

- Before discussing individual essays, spend some time with your class answering Rothenberg's question in her introduction: "Why . . . do so many people, in particular, so many young people, seem to believe that racism and sexism are largely things of the past?" Do or did your students feel this way? Why? Why is it easier to think this way than to see discrimination as an ongoing problem facing Americans? Have their feelings changed since doing the reading in this part? How?

- "The Problem: Discrimination," a 1981 report, usefully outlines three levels of discrimination in the United States. Spend time with students discussing the definitions of these levels. Does this piece help students map out the ways discrimination functions structurally and systemically in American society? How?

- Devote some time to talking about the differences between intentional and unintentional racism, sexism, homophobia, and so on. What constitutes intentional? What constitutes unintentional? Are people who commit unintentional acts off the hook? Why or why not? How do people become aware of their own biases and try to address them in order to avoid committing hurtful acts of prejudice?

- Is striving for a "color-blind" or "gender-neutral" society the solution for the problems outlined in Part III? Why or why not? What do both of those terms imply? Do they eliminate racism and sexism? Or do they sidestep racism and sexism? What other solutions might there be for dealing with institutional and individual discriminatory practices and attitudes?

- Have students read the newspaper or watch or listen to the news every day to monitor acts of discrimination. What do they see or hear when they do this? Ask them not only to read about and watch for incidents but also to pay attention to how the stories are written or reported on. Remind them that the media is another institution that has potential for discrimination built into it. What are journalists' assumptions and biases when they report a story? What is their worldview, their own ideological perspective? Whose side do they seem to be on?

ASSIGNMENTS

Generating Ideas/Small-Group Discussions

ASSIGNMENT 1. "The Problem: Discrimination," a 1981 report by the U.S. Commission on Civil Rights, outlines three systemic levels of discriminatory practices, individual, organizational, and structural (III, 22). By breaking discrimination into three levels, the report's authors are trying to make distinctions between various practices and also complicate events to avoid any sort of easy answers. Your instructor will split the class into several small groups; with your group members, discuss one of the examples in the article all the way through its three levels. After you have done this, choose an article from Part III that lends itself to this sort of systemic analysis. Reconvene with the rest of the class and discuss your examples.

ASSIGNMENT 2. For homework, write one to two pages in which you discuss how one of the pieces in Part III either did or did not help you visualize one of the concepts explored in Parts I and II. How do real-life examples aid people in understanding the ways various forms of oppressions manifest themselves? How does the event or situation in your article illustrate the ways socially constructed identities can be harmful?

ASSIGNMENT 3. Your instructor will break the class into small groups. Each group will choose a reading from Part III and, using a concept or term from Part II, discuss what form or forms of discrimination the incident in the reading manifests. Group members should also talk about what interested them particularly about the reading—why did they choose it? Each group should present its discussion to the rest of the class.

ASSIGNMENT 4. As a class, using "The Problem: Discrimination" (III, 22), categorize the readings in Part III to understand how patterns of discrimination operate in this society. Why, for example, do you think there are several articles about hate crimes and stereotyping? Or about discriminatory hiring practices? Or about financial inequalities? How does power operate in and through institutions?

Writing Assignments

ASSIGNMENT 5. Read "Asian American Journalists Association Objects to Syndicated Cartoonist's Use of Racist Stereotypes of Asians" (III, 30) and "Asian American" by Sonia Shah (V, 62). In an essay, analyze some of the stereotypes surrounding Asian Americans. On the one hand, following the article about racist cartoons in Part III, what are some traditional stereotypes associated with Asian people? Where did they come from, do you think? On the other hand, why are Asian Americans also termed the "model minority"? What does Shah mean when she states that: "While an education can be had and a living made based on model minority myths (at least for some), it is at the cost of indulging the racist delusion that there can be some 'good minorities' in implicit contrast to those other 'bad minorities,' who have only themselves to blame"? You might also look at Janice Mirikitani's poem, "Suicide Note" (V, 63), which is written from the perspective of a young woman who kills herself because she doesn't achieve a perfect academic record. Mirikitani outlines the brutality inherent in the "model minority" stereotype when someone internalizes its oppressive implications. What consequences do all of these depictions have for Asian Americans and for their relationships with other ethnic groups?

ASSIGNMENT 6. After reading "Study Finds the Nation's Public School Districts Are Resegregating by Race" by Jay Lindsay (III, 40) and "Are America's Schools Leaving Latinas Behind?", a report by the American Association of University Women (III, 42), write about the implications of a built-in disparity among children in American schools. Analyze the article and perhaps draw on current discussions concerning school reform, such as vouchers, charter schools, and the like. Do you think such programs will work? Why or why not?

ASSIGNMENT 7. Several of the articles in Part III reveal rampant sexism, sexual harassment, and racial discrimination at some of the United States' most revered businesses, such as Wal-Mart and Denny's. These businesses often rely on low-wage workers to run their operations. What do you make of such hostile work environments? Write a paper in which you first outline the causes of such discriminatory practices, the practices themselves, and some possible solutions. Could the nature of the work foster such behavior? Why or why not, do you think?

ASSIGNMENT 8. The articles in Part III all deal with discrimination that affects the most central aspects of people's lives: mobility, work, sexuality, education, finances, home, safety, and the like. If you are going into a helping profession such as social work, counseling, nursing, or teaching, how does being aware of the pervasive aspects of discrimination help you think about the people you will be dealing with? What insights can you glean from the readings in this part of the text? Make sure to cite some specific examples from the articles to support your exploration.

Research/Analysis Projects

ASSIGNMENT 9. Research the history of the term "civil rights" and analyze it. What does the term mean? What does it have to do with a democratic society? Make sure to cite specific examples to illustrate your points.

ASSIGNMENT 10. After reading the articles in Part III, you are probably becoming more aware of how pervasive discrimination of all kinds is in our society today. Taking Part III as a jumping-off point, research and analyze a story about discrimination that has happened recently. You may choose to focus on a local event or on one that was reported nationally (like hate crimes against Muslims in the wake of 9/11, which you can also refer to in the article "Anti-Muslim Crimes Jump After Sept. 11 in Jersey and U.S." [II, 29] in this part). In your paper, make sure to note not just what happened and what you think it means but also how the story was reported.

ASSIGNMENT 11. The two articles "EEOC Sues Arizona Diner for National Origin Bias Against Navajos and Other Native Americans" (III, 31) and "Students Defend Icon That Offends" by Sam McManis (III, 45) detail some of the entrenched inequities Native American still confront in contemporary U.S. society. While many will view the incidents in the first article with some outrage, they will often dismiss the concerns detailed in the second. In a paper, research the controversy surrounding the use of Native American images as team mascots. What are your attitudes towards this practice? Why do you think the way you do? How are the incidents outlined in these two articles linked, do you think?

ASSIGNMENT 12. Research an issue surrounding affirmative action. In the last few years, citizens in some states, such as California, have voted in mandates to end affirmative action on the state and local levels. Schools such as the University of Texas have eliminated affirmative action admissions policies. In these cases, the justification for the actions was that affirmative action no longer worked. At the same time, the University of Michigan's law school is under attack, by President George W. Bush no less, for holding on to its admissions policies that utilize race and ethnicity as an enhancement for admittance to its school. Is affirmative action still necessary? Why or why not, in your view? What does your research show? What do the articles in Part III demonstrate? Is the "playing field" now "leveled" enough to give equal access to well-paying jobs and educational opportunities to women and minorities? Why or why not? Be sure to carefully document your sources and to draw from a variety of well-researched perspectives.

ASSIGNMENT 13. While several of the articles in Part III focus on class inequities, especially as they intersect with race and gender, a few show that even in the middle and upper classes, inequities with regard to gender still exist. After reading the articles "Equality at Work Remains Elusive" by Rachel Smolkin (III, 25), "Tee Time for Equality" by Deborah Rhode (III, 37), and "The All-Boy Network: Public Affairs Shows Reflect Shortage of Women in Power" by Howard Kurtz (III, 43), analyze the pervasive aspects of gender discrimination. Do some research on recent statistics to support your discussion. How far have women come? Has there been retrenchment with regard to equality of late? Why?

ASSIGNMENT 14. How does the media contribute to the maintenance of inequalities? Pick a category such as race, class, gender, sexuality, etc., and analyze how television deals with it. Survey recent TV shows—sitcoms, dramas, news shows—and collect data on the ways the media represents these categories. You might look at Howard Kurtz's article on women in public affairs shows (III, 43) or Matt Zoller's piece on minorities in television (III, 44) for guidance on this project.

RECOMMENDED MEDIA

- CBS, ABC, and NBC news shows have all done various stories documenting day-to-day racial discrimination. You might consult the networks' websites to find videotapes of those shows.

- Most of the stories in Part III are from newspaper and magazine articles. Survey a couple of newspapers and magazines, or have your students pay attention to media sources, to bring in more stories to class. This will keep the material constantly up to date; at the same time, it will show that the stories in this part do not represent isolated incidents but, rather, ongoing problems.

- You might go over your school's code of conduct and sexual harassment policies in class. Why are these regulations in place? What do they demonstrate to students about what the climate was for non-privileged people in the past?

- Compare and contrast the ways race, ethnicity, gender, sexuality, class, bias, discrimination, etc. are reported on Fox News or MSNBC versus the pieces in Part III. Videotape segments from these channels and bring them in for your class to analyze. How do the frameworks of these networks impact the way they deliver information?

- Have your students check out an alternative news website such as www.cursor.org. You might also have them look at Fairness and Accuracy In Reporting's website (www.fair.org) and newsletter. These sources generally have a vastly different take on important news items than the major news media. Have students compare and contrast these sources.

PART IV

The Economics of Race, Class, and Gender in the United States

In Part IV, Rothenberg details the ways economics intersects with race, ethnicity, and gender to determine how people will be able to live their lives. Countering notions that poor people are poor because they are "naturally" less able, the essays in this part quite specifically outline recent economic trends that impact middle-class, working-class, working-poor, and poor people's lives in a myriad of ways. The essays here discuss how economic standing can affect the most basic aspects of our lives: relationships with each other, health, access to education, feelings of self-worth, and the ways we raise our children. When one factors in race or gender issues, these aspects can be significantly altered. For example, people of color who have attained middle-class standing might still be segregated in low-income neighborhoods because of the color of their skin, and women of all races who need public assistance are time and time again stigmatized as lazy, slovenly, and ignorant (although the combination of gender and race in discussions of welfare create truly racist and oppressive stereotypes). These essays will be helpful for students in that they present a wealth of information, both statistical and personal. The mix of well-researched data and narratives about personal economic experiences simultaneously prevents students from dismissing these issues as mere "opinion" and also humanizes damaging constructions of working-class, working-poor, and poor people. At the same time, discussions of middle-class issues show students from that socioeconomic level that their lives are not as secure as they might have believed; indeed, that they might have more in common with people below them on the economic ladder than with those above.

ISSUES AND QUESTIONS TO CONSIDER

- What is "middle class"? Are we a country of middle-class people? Or are we a classless society? What *is* class, then?

- Holly Sklar, in "Imagine a Country—2003," cites a number of problems that occur in the United States, and points out the contradiction that the richest country in the world has such troubles. Many students, though, become frustrated that Sklar names the problems but does not propose any solutions. They can be overwhelmed by the amount of information she provides. Discuss with them why this might be so. Does their experience with information sources provide them with detailed information about the world in which they live? What sorts of information do they have access to regarding economics in this country? Whose interests does the media represent? And, finally, why doesn't Sklar provide solutions to the numerous problems she names? Is that her job?

- How does race factor into economics? Spend some time going over statistics in "The Wage Gap: Myths and Facts" by the National Committee on Pay Equity and in Conley's discussion of the wealth gap between white and minority families. Does everyone have an equal chance to make a lot of money in this country? Also look at the profiles that Mantsios constructs in Part II. Why does one person have so much more opportunity than the others in the essay?

- Discuss the work ethic and the American dream. What do students think these things are? Students will probably be particularly vociferous about "Billionaire's Ex-Wife Wants $4,400 a Day to Raise Daughter," which should lead to some interesting discussions about the work ethic. This is especially true if you then look at Newman's article on the working poor in Harlem or Crenshaw's article on women's financial instability upon retirement. Are the people these authors talk about "lazy"? Do they lack an American dream? What prevents them from achieving their dreams? How is it that government assistance has been demonized when it goes to the poor but not when it goes to the rich? What do myths about people who "make it" because of "hard work" (such as those about Andrew Carnegie or Horatio Alger) do to discussions of poverty and people who live impoverished existences? How do they serve to socially construct attitudes and stereotypes of the poor and maintain economic hierarchies by preventing discussions of the redistribution of wealth? You might ask students to think about Krugman's article on political dynasties and inherited wealth. How does this piece illuminate this discussion?

- Have a discussion about work and gender. Crenshaw's article on women's insecurity details the ways women can be financially vulnerable when they retire even if they've worked most of their lives. Many students—women in particular—might want to argue that they can "make it" if they work hard enough, that they won't have to rely on their husband's salaries, and that they won't have economic barriers when they begin—or end—their careers. This is a tough position to counter because many women students have such high hopes for themselves. It's important, then, to keep focused on systemic and structural issues surrounding economics and work, rather than on individual stories of achievement.

- Malveaux and Krugman make points about the economics of the Bush administration and the war on terror. You could ask your students how they view the class status of many members of the Bush administration (including Bush himself), the administration's economic policies, and the economic future of the country. Do they think there is a connection? What is it? What purpose does Krugman's article serve in reminding people that an upper class exists, that one's entrance into it is largely through inheritance, and that the people who hold the highest offices are often members of it?

ASSIGNMENTS

Generating Ideas/Small-Group Discussions

ASSIGNMENT 1. Read Holly Sklar's essay (IV, 47) and in a small group, brainstorm some solutions to three of the problems she names. When the class gets back together, discuss the problems your group identified, why you chose to focus on those particular problems, and the solutions your group came up with. How does thinking about solutions alter the way you read the Sklar text? Is it helpful? How does her use of research and statistics add or detract from her overall point? Why are statistics important?

ASSIGNMENT 2. In your journal, consider the differences in lifestyle between Irene LaMarche in "Her Next Step" by Albert B. Crenshaw (IV, 54) and Patricia Duff in "Billionaire's Ex-Wife Wants $4,400 a Day to Raise Daughter" by David Rohde (IV, 55). While many people would be astonished at the amounts of money Duff feels she needs to have "parity" with her ex-husband, some would argue that that is the life this woman is used to and, therefore, that she should have it. However, very often no such compassion exists in the same way for women in LaMarche's position. When women's husbands or even ex-husbands die, and their livelihoods depend on that second salary, they are in a very precarious position. The question here is whether there should be such disparity in how people live their lives. What economic stability can people expect? Is it fair that there is such a gap between the rich and the poor, or even between the rich and the middle class? Consider this quote from Robert Pear's article, "Number of People Living in Poverty Increases in U.S." (IV, 48): "The most affluent fifth of the population received half of all household income last year, up from 45 percent in 1985. The poorest fifth received 3.5 percent of total household income, down from 4 percent in 1985." With whom do you sympathize: Irene LaMarche and the other women mentioned in Crenshaw's article, or Patricia Duff? Is it equitable that one household should be squabbling over so much money while another will probably not be able to bring in enough to pay the bills and the mortgage? What's the answer?

ASSIGNMENT 3. Many of the articles in Part IV ask that you examine economics in the United States from a structural perspective: there are stagnant home ownership rates among people of color in comparison to growth rates among whites; there is still a persistent gap in earning between whites and people of color despite class level; poor and professional women alike are limited in terms of work and economics because of their gender; and wealth and power have become even more concentrated in the upper classes. Choose one of the articles in Part IV and, with a partner, map out the ways race and/or gender intersect with economics and how those intersections affect people's lives. For instance, if you look at "Being Black, Living in the Red: Wealth Matters" (IV, 51), how does Conley chart the differences between two families with similar income levels? After you and your partner have drawn the map, first take a moment with your partner to think about the implications of the system the two of you have outlined and then consider solutions. What can be done to control for race and/or gender and to close the gap between the haves and the have-nots in a structural and systemic manner? Try to avoid individualized solutions in your deliberations.

ASSIGNMENT 4. As a homework assignment or a page in your journal, discuss your aspirations for your economic future. Where do you think your desires came from? What do you want for yourself? What is your work ethic? Is it enough in the face of current economic trends? This assignment is not meant to burst your bubble or critique your aspirations but to help you see how you fit in the larger economic landscape: to see yourself as part of a larger structure. Think about yourself both as an individual and as part of a greater whole. How might society structure itself differently to help more people realize their potential? Does your gender, race, ethnicity, or sexual orientation affect what you see for yourself in the future?

Writing Assignments

ASSIGNMENT 5. Draw on your brainstorming session about problems in Sklar's article (IV, 47) in order to write an essay about two or three issues your group discussed. What are *your* solutions to Sklar's problems? What would your world look like? How might you "imagine" a better country? If you want to argue against some of Sklar's points, how do you interpret her identification of problems differently? What counterarguments might you offer?

ASSIGNMENT 6. Using at least two of the essays in Part IV, write an essay on the American dream. What is it? Who has access to it? Is it a positive, useful myth? Or is it detrimental to people? You might draw on some of the statistics Pear (IV, 48), Malveaux (IV, 50), and the National Committee on Pay Equity (IV, 53) cite, and then look at a personal narrative such as Kim Phillips-Fein's piece on Jessica Rivera (IV, 56). It is up to you, however, to decide which essays you will draw on.

ASSIGNMENT 7. After reviewing Kim Phillips-Fein's "The Education of Jessica Rivera" (IV, 56), discuss your views of welfare and social services for the poor. Are they necessary? Why or why not? Do societies have a responsibility toward their citizens if their citizens have need? Why or why not? Would you replace welfare with something else? What do you think has happened in this country as a result of the state and federal welfare "reforms" of a few years ago? What is the image of people on welfare? How do you think this came into being? How does welfare fit into the larger capitalist structure of the United States?

Research/Analysis Projects

ASSIGNMENT 8. What sorts of stereotypes exist about poor women? Poor people? How do poor people view themselves, and why? Draw on Katherine S. Newman's observations about the working poor in Harlem for your discussion (IV, 57) and Kim Phillips-Fein's piece about Jessica Rivera and her struggles to obtain an education (IV, 56). As Newman puts it, do these people lack a proper "work ethic"? How does an impoverished existence make one more vulnerable to things like abuse, domestic violence, and unsafe and crowded living conditions? Can it be that people's fear of the urban, fear of poverty, and fear of the "other" has ties to economic conditions? What do you think? Write an essay in which you discuss several of these issues. You might research some particular connections, such as those between domestic violence and poverty. Or you might examine someone's study of an area, such as Newman's, and discuss the social implications of the study. What does it reveal about the ways economics determines or constructs people's lives and their sense of possibility for the future? Or you can survey a week's worth of media—TV, magazines, or newspapers—for representations of poor people. What sorts of stereotypes are perpetuated? What is the reality behind such stereotyping?

ASSIGNMENT 9. Go out and do your own research on two or three of the problems Sklar details in her essay (IV, 47). How have other countries in the world dealt with these problems? Are their solutions different from the solutions pursued in the United States? Spend some time comparing differing approaches and then identify which ones you think work best and why.

ASSIGNMENT 10. After reading the articles in Part IV—especially "Number of People Living in Poverty Increases in U.S." (IV, 48) and "The Wage Gap: Myths and Facts" (IV, 53)—turn to Part VIII and read "Narrowing the Income Gap Between Rich and Poor" (VIII, 123), in which Michael Hout and Samuel R. Lucas argue that a solution to this problem (among others) is a revitalized labor union movement. Also be sure to look at "A Clean Sweep: The SEIU's Organizing Drive for Janitors Shows How Unionization Can Raise Wages" by Harold Meyerson (VIII, 124). Write a research paper in which you discuss what unions can and cannot do for working people. You might do some research on the history of the labor movement, on a particular industry or strike, or on a specific leader. As the authors have asked you to do throughout this text, however, avoid easy answers and stereotyping. Really dig in and investigate why Hout and Lucas make the claim that they do in their article.

ASSIGNMENT 11. After reading Malveaux's (IV, 50) and Krugman's (IV, 52) pieces, write a research paper in which you analyze the economics of the war on terror. How much has it cost? How has it affected the rest of the federal budget? The state budgets? What do you make of this? Is it a necessary expenditure? Why or why not, in your opinion? In your essay, be sure to outline the history of the war on terror along with its economic impact.

RECOMMENDED MEDIA

- Show a documentary that depicts either a historical or a contemporary labor issue, such as *Miles of Smiles, Years of Struggle: The Untold Story of the Black Pullman Porter; The Fight in the Fields: Cesar Chavez and the United Farm Workers; With Babies and Banners* (which is about women's roles in the 1930s sit-down strikes at General Motors); *American Dream* (about a strike at a Hormel meat-packing plant); or *Harlan County, USA* (about a coal miners' strike in West Virginia in the 1970s). How do labor unions or collective labor consciousness help workers? You may have to spend some time breaking through students' misconceptions of unions. These films are a good way to get them thinking from the perspective of workers, rather than from that of owners and managers.

- Along these same lines, show John Sayles's fictional film *Matewan*, which tells the story of a miners' strike in a small town in West Virginia in the 1920s. The film deals with issues of both race and gender along with economics and is an engaging way to show students the multiple intersections, within a historical context, of these axes.

- Show either *Roger and Me* or *The Big One*, both by Michael Moore. You can also refer students to Moore's website. Moore's humorous and satirical portrayals of the plight of working people in this country translate well for students, and Moore consistently turns the tables on those in power rather than on the powerless.

- For an early comedic look at working people's lives, show Charlie Chaplin's *Modern Times*. You might discuss the treatment of working people and also how workers represent their own lives.

- You might also present a slide show of documentary photographers' work on the poor, such as that of Lewis Hine in the early part of the twentieth century and the photography of Farm Security Administration artists in the thirties like Walker Evans and Dorothea Lange (known for her famous "Dust Bowl Madonna" photo). Discuss the social value of depicting poverty. You might tie this discussion to Mantsios's piece in Part VII on "Media Magic." What can people learn from seeing "how the other half lives"? What drawbacks might there be to this kind of work?

- For a humorous but extremely informative video, show PBS's *Affluenza*, which discusses the consequences of rampant consumerism in America and its ties to class and wealth. What do students think about the filmmakers' conclusions and solutions?

- Be sure to show the recent PBS documentary on class, *People Like Us*. This video, which combines satire with hard statistics, is one of the best, most accessible discussions of class in America. It covers issues of race and ethnicity, gender, food, and social practices. It also does not avoid detailing the lives of the upper classes, thus giving students a full view of status—or lack thereof—in the United States today.

PART V

Many Voices, Many Lives: Some Consequences of Racial, Gender, and Class Inequality

The power of many of the personal accounts in Part V stems not only from their expressions of the pain and conflict in others' lives but also from our general lack of familiarity with other people's points of view. Students tend to respond strongly to this part of the book; the authors' personal narratives concretize the more abstract concepts from other parts, often in gripping ways. Thus, Part V can provide you with powerful tools for encouraging students to think through the experiences of inequity, both in terms of their own lives and in terms of being sensitive to the conflicts others must live through. The consequences of social hierarchies are not abstract, and they are not purely perceptual (that is, thinking differently about them won't make them go away). They are material, and the operations of race, class, gender, and sexual hierarchies can be observed in all aspects of day-to-day living. Several of these selections emphasize the ways that everyday details reveal the structures governing our lives, if we look carefully enough. But the personal focus in this part often leads students to individualize the problems the text has tried to emphasize as being systemic, *social* dilemmas. This is not to say that individuals don't experience these issues; they do, obviously. However, in thinking through these issues only from an individual perspective (which is what many students do early on in their educational careers), students can miss the big picture. The assignments in Part V are designed to keep students focused on the social framework as they respond to the essays. Many of the assignments, in fact, ask them to literally read the essays here through a lens constructed by something from elsewhere in the book.

ISSUES AND QUESTIONS TO CONSIDER

- Review the census figures for 2000 and discus the implications of the findings. What does it mean that America is more diverse?

- Ask students to identify moments in the readings in which daily life reveals social hierarchies. How effective is this device in conveying the pervasiveness of race, class, gender, and sexual constructions (Wu, Jimenez, Mirikitani, Sabo, Shange, Cofer, for example)?

- Part V, more than any other, is the place to demonstrate the ways in which privilege functions as loss; privilege can permit us and deny us all sorts of knowledge. Cofer illustrates this point beautifully when she discusses how stereotypes of Latinas prevent people of other ethnicities from knowing the incredible richness not only of her Puerto Rican roots but also of the whole range of cultures that compose the Latin American world. Ask students what their socially constructed point of view permits them to see and what it keeps them from seeing. In other words, how does their subjectivity as a particularly raced, classed, gendered (and so on) person enable them to see or prevent them from seeing how other people experience their lives?

- Does self-understanding assist in self-transformation or not (Wood, Avicolli, Bornstein)?

- What do these selections suggest about the possibilities for changing the racist and sexist attitudes of others? What is the role of education as a solution for ending racism (Shah, El Sawy, Wood, Wu)? Sexism (Cofer, Avicolli, Gerhart, Mann, Chung, Griscom)? What is the significance of political action, and what conditions give rise to an individual's political involvement (El Sawy, Kochiyama, Shah, Copeland, Terkel)?

- Class, gender, race, and ethnicity do not map across each other in neat, predictable ways. Several selections underscore how complicated these intersections can be. How does class position shift the significance of one's gender (Jordan)? One's race or ethnicity (Mirikitani, Cofer, Wise)?

- How does a person of mixed heritage expose the lie of racial categories? How does the notion of racial purity complicate racial identity ("America 2000: A Map of the Mix," Alsultany, Chung)?

- The constructed nature of sexuality can be seen most readily when we resist the constructions and when we try to make visible the codes of masculinity, femininity, and heterosexuality. Students may benefit from reviewing Part I to address this question (Cofer, Sabo, Avicolli, Copeland, Gerhart, Bornstein).

- Spend some time discussing masculinity and violence with your students. How do they define each other in many ways (Sabo, Jordan)? How do race and class intersect with violence and masculinity (Wise)?

- Because many of the essays in this section are stories, you might spend some time with the class discussing the role of narration in the construction of people's lives. How do the authors "write" themselves?

ASSIGNMENTS

Generating Ideas/Small-Group Discussions

ASSIGNMENT 1. Many of the essays in this section draw attention to the fact that they are stories, narratives of their authors' lives. How do we create our own lives through the stories we tell about ourselves? How can we "author" our lives? How can't we? And how do our stories of our pasts influence the way we live presently? Consider these questions in your journal, and bring your answers to class.

ASSIGNMENT 2. Go over "Census 2000 Shows America's Diversity" (V, 58) and "America 2000: A Map of the Mix" (V, 59). Why do you think these selections are included in the portion of *Race, Class, and Gender in the United States* devoted to personal accounts? What do the different experiences of each racial and ethnic group suggest about racial categories in the United States? Consider Omi and Winant's argument in relation to this selection (I, 1). Think about these questions for 10 minutes. Take notes on a sheet of paper, then meet with others in a small group to discuss your answers.

ASSIGNMENT 3. Read Sabo's "Pigskin, Patriarchy, and Pain" (V, 70), Avicolli's "He Defies You Still" (V, 71), and Sanday's "Pulling Train" (VII, 110); review Lorber's "'Night to His Day': The Social Construction of Gender" (I, 5), Kimmel's "Masculinity as Homophobia" (I, 8), and Johnson's "Patriarchy" (II, 17). What is masculinity? How do masculinity and patriarchy intersect? How does masculinity depend on homosexuality for its definition? How do stereotypes of homosexual behavior support the belief that homosexuality and masculinity are in contradiction? How does homosexuality seemingly (but not actually) interfere with the construction of masculinity? How do some of these authors experience their masculinity? Consider these questions in a journal entry.

ASSIGNMENT 4. With others in a small group, survey all of Part V and decide which piece the group members all liked the best. Choose someone to take notes, and discuss the article. What about it was compelling to you? What did the members of your group learn from it? How does it tie into previous parts of the text? How does it tie into previous essays in the text? The group should share its discussion with the rest of the class.

ASSIGNMENT 5. Read June Jordan's "Requiem for the Champ" (V, 73). In a journal entry, consider Jordan's use of words such as "winning" and "fighting." What have these words come to mean for her? What is she concerned with? What does "requiem" mean and why has Jordan written one? What perspective on economic success does she offer that the sports hero stories overlook? Be sure to take into account the analyses of masculinity, athleticism, and violence provided by Sabo (V, 70) and Kimmel (I, 8).

ASSIGNMENT 6. Read the interview with C. P. Ellis conducted by Studs Terkel (V, 82). Ellis comes to understand the role that racial hierarchies play in maintaining class hierarchies, and it is through this understanding that he begins to dismantle his racism. Seemingly minor episodes, such as walking down a street, were the basis for his self-understanding and transformation. Identify the moments when Ellis first begins to see the social structures that organize his life. What can one learn from Ellis's transformation? Consider these issues for about 15 minutes. Take notes on a sheet of paper, then meet in a small group to discuss your answers.

ASSIGNMENT 7. Part V illustrates the many ways in which the ordinary episodes of daily life are affected by the social constructions of race, ethnicity, class, gender, sexuality, and ability. It might seem as though these details are informed by personal choice, but consider instead how one's class and gender position affect these so-called choices. Working in a pair, consider the details of your daily lives: attempt to map the categories of race, ethnicity, class, sexuality, gender, and ability across them. For example, does class influence your selection of foods? Your clothing? Your hobbies and interests? Does your race or ethnicity affect what school you attend and what careers are available to you? Do they influence how and where you spend your summers? Does your gender affect what you choose to study at college or which sports you participate in? When your class reconvenes, compare your pair's comments and observations with those of the other pairs.

Writing Assignments

ASSIGNMENT 8. For people going into "helping professions" such as teaching, social work, or counseling, listening openly and compassionately to other people's stories is important work. Really paying attention not only to how people narrate their lives but also to what individual experiences they have had will enable you to challenge your assumptions about people different from yourself. In an essay, choose one or more of the pieces from Part V and discuss how you might use the insights the author conveys to you. What can you learn from listening to how someone tells her or his story? How might this help you in your later work helping others? What assumptions did you discover you needed to challenge? How were they challenged?

ASSIGNMENT 9. Cofer describes what it is like to be treated as "a character" in a "cartoon-populated universe" (V, 66). Several selections in Part V (Wu, Shah, Shaheen, El Sawy, Cofer, Chung, Gerhart) demonstrate one's inability to escape entirely the effects of media-generated race and gender stereotypes, regardless of one's class position or education level. In an essay, trace the effects of race and gender stereotypes through these selections and others in the book and in your own life. As an added dimension to your analysis, consider Paul's (VII, 106) and Miller's (I, 11) arguments for the self-fulfilling nature of stereotypes. What coping mechanisms do people devise? What conclusions can you draw about identity? How much of *who* we are is socially constructed?

ASSIGNMENT 10. Read Griscom's "The Case of Kowalski and Thompson: Ableism, Heterosexism, and Sexism" (V, 79) and Davies's "Lame" (V, 80). In both articles, the authors take care to articulate the interlocking strands of social resistance, the multiple modes of oppression that disabled women suffer. Write an essay in which you describe the three modes of oppression endured by Kowalski, Thompson, and Davies. Define ableism, heterosexism, and sexism, and describe how these combine to create additional obstacles in the women's lives. What do the non-disabled take for granted? What do you make of Davies's use of the term "lame" to describe herself? Why does she do this? How do the fears of disability mirror the fears and ignorance of homosexuality? Are the three oppressions similar, or do they differ? You may want to review Baynton's "Disability and the Justification of Inequality in American History" (I, 9), Frye's "Oppression" (II, 18) and Ettelbrick's "Confronting Obstacles to Lesbian and Gay Equality" (VI, 105).

Research/Analysis Projects

ASSIGNMENT 11. Consider Don Sabo's "Pigskin, Patriarchy, and Pain" (V, 70) and Ann Gerhart's "More and More Young Women Choose Surgical 'Perfection'" (V, 77), and write a paper in which you explore the costs of gender construction. You might collect ads or fashion layouts from magazines such as *Glamour, Mademoiselle, Seventeen, Elle,* and the like, and compare them to sports figures in *Sports Illustrated* or male models in *GQ, Details,* or *Maxim.* How are femininity and masculinity constructed through the media? What ideal is presented to people? How is that ideal achieved? What are the costs? At the end of your paper, discuss the implications of your findings for future generations. Are we headed down a "healthy" path? Why or why not?

ASSIGNMENT 12. Using Kochiyama's oral history "Then Came the War" (V, 60), research Japanese internment in World War II and write a paper about it. Was this action justified? Why or why not? You might also look at El Sawy's piece "Yes, I Follow Islam, but I'm Not a Terrorist" (V, 65) and think about the current context in the United States in the wake of the September 11, 2001 terrorist attacks in New York and Washington, D.C., the ensuing "war on terror," and the 2003 commencement of a war against Iraq. How close is the United States currently to replicating with Arab Americans or people of the Muslim faith what happened during World War II to Japanese Americans? Is the loss of civil liberties to this extent ever justified? Why or why not? What do the terms "freedom" and "liberty" mean, then? How does an event such as 9/11 strip away social conventions and allow people to act on their fears? (You might look at the article in Part III on the jump in hate crimes against Muslims to think about this question). You could look up the Patriot Act, which was passed by Congress right after September 11, 2001, in order to provide even more context for some of these difficult questions.

ASSIGNMENT 13. Interview one or more family members to create your own oral history on the subject of race or class relations. Ask your subjects to relate as many details of their lives as possible to help you understand the period of time they are describing. How do they explain their beliefs and actions? Have those beliefs changed? How do they explain those changes? Were the changes the result of dramatic events, or did they come through a slow process of "unlearning"?

ASSIGNMENT 14. Your task in this assignment is to reflect on yourself in relation to others—in this case, other texts in *Race, Class, and Gender in the United States.* Write an essay in which you "narrate yourself." To do this, select a seemingly minor moment from your past (such as a conversation with a family member or an encounter with a stranger) that encapsulates within it some feature of your life whose significance you may not have understood at the time or may still need to figure out. You may use one episode or a series of small events. It can be a dream, a conversation, or a routine part of your day. The point is to select some moment or set of moments through which you've come to understand the significance of your place in the race, class, and gender hierarchies that organize your daily life. How are the material conditions of your life shaped by your place in the social scheme? Draw on selections from Part V to help you clarify your experiences. "Narrating yourself" in this assignment means "you, in relation to your social and cultural context."

RECOMMENDED MEDIA

- Pair a popular film that students will be familiar with, such as *Raiders of the Lost Ark* or something more recent, with Shaheen's "TV Arabs" (V, 353). Ask students to identify ways in which Arabs are represented and to decide whether this confirms Shaheen's argument about the representation of Arabs in the American cultural imagination. Show this film with *Faces of the Enemy*, directed by Sam Keen, to further illustrate the media's role in demonizing groups we deem "the enemy." (The video has a book that accompanies it.) You could also ask students to name who the "enemies" are in current thrillers. Are they "Americans"? Or are they "others"? What sorts of "others" do they tend to be?

- Show John Sayles's *Lone Star*. This film is useful for illustrating the intersections of family history with community history and what those intersections reveal about race and gender categories. Trace each story line. How does the film help students understand the way racial categories are maintained? What does the film say about borders? About racial mixing? What do students make of the ending? How can it be read as metaphorical?

- Show *Smoke Signals*, which is a kind of contemporary vision quest for its main character. Discuss what the film does with Native American stereotyping. What does the main character learn by the end of the film? You could also pair this film with clips from the recently released *Windtalkers*, a film starring Nicholas Cage that supposedly details the experiences of Navajos who were enlisted in the military during World War II to create a new code based on their language. Have students read the article in Part III on Navajos being discriminated against for speaking their own language in their place of work and then discuss that in relation to these two films. What stereotypes does *Windtalkers* rely on to tell its story? How does *Smoke Signals* challenge those stereotypes?

- Show *Return to Paradise*, a Hollywood-ized love story between a Japanese American woman being held in an internment camp and a white soldier. You might also refer students to the Manzanar website for historical background on Japanese American internment. How much do students know about this period in American history? How successful have efforts been to recover this history?

- Show *Mississippi Masala* and discuss how the film deals with interethnic issues.

- You could also show *Tortilla Soup* as a light-hearted look at a Mexican American family negotiating with the contemporary world. Have students look for the ways the film deals not just with ethnicity, but also gender—especially in the opening scenes where it is the patriarch of the family who makes a huge meal for his daughters. Other films that deal with Mexican American life in the United States include *My Family*, and *Mi Vida Loca (My Crazy Life)*, which explores gang life from a girl's perspective.

- For a light-hearted look at the dysfunctionality of suburban families, you might show an episode of Comedy Central's cartoon series *South Park* and have students analyze what the makers of the series are spoofing.

- Finally, pair Tim Wise's piece on school shootings with Michael Moore's Academy Award-winning documentary *Bowling for Columbine*, which has a searing analysis of gun violence, class, and race in the United States, all told through Moore's vintage brand of slapstick humor and biting commentary.

PART VI

How It Happened: Race and Gender Issues in U.S. Law

Part VI is an invaluable section in that it demonstrates to students how race, class, gender, and sexuality have been institutionalized and regulated throughout the history of the United States. Because this part is composed almost entirely of legal documents such as texts of laws, court decisions, and the like, it is one of the most flexible in the book. It particularly lends itself to research projects, as these documents appear without specific historical context. You may also choose to assign isolated selections to accompany other readings in the book (such as Kochiyama [V, 60] with *Korematsu* v. *United States*). The absence of historical context can be a classroom virtue because you can ask students to think of these selections as constituting a "text" that critiques the notion of American justice as applied to women, people of color, and non-heterosexuals. You can also have students go out and do their own research to provide the historical context for particular documents. Because this critique is available from the words of the documents themselves, students will find irrefutable evidence for the history of oppression in this country. Remind students that these documents are not ancient history and that many of these courtroom battles are still being fought in various ways.

ISSUES AND QUESTIONS TO CONSIDER

- What are the conditions for citizenship, as revealed in these documents (*Dred Scott* v. *Sandford*, "The Black Codes," the California Constitution, *People* v. *Hall*)? How does this portrait compare with the essays in Part II?

- Trace the notion of justice as it appears in the documents in Part VI. Whom is the Supreme Court actually protecting in cases such as *People* v. *Hall*, *Korematsu* v. *United States*, and *Elk* v. *Wilkins*?

- Many people believe that women have only very recently fought for their rights. However, the sheer number of court cases and legal rulings on the rights of women suggests that women have worked hard for legal and social equality for over a century. Given the number of cases addressing the rights of women, does it appear that women have been content with their legally prescribed role? Whose interest does the narrative of "recent change" serve? What do the documents in this part suggest? (See "Declaration of Sentiments and Resolutions, 1848"; "The Anti-Suffragists: Selected Papers, 1852–1887"; *Minor v. Happersett*, 1874; *Bradwell v. Illinois*, 1873; United States Constitution: Nineteenth Amendment, 1920; *Roe v. Wade*, 1973; the Equal Rights Amendment).

- How significant is the right to vote? Does it matter that the right to vote has been denied to over half the population for most of the United States' history (See the Fifteenth and Nineteenth Amendments)?

- What should the constitution protect? What does "equal protection under the law" mean (Ettelbrick)?

- Ask students to review Holly Sklar's "Imagine a Country" in Part IV in light of the materials in Part VI. Did they know that the United States was a country whose legal history enabled so many human and civil rights abuses? Have the documents in Part VI caused them to think differently about the notion of justice?

- Given the historical inequities contained herein, discuss some current legal issues, such as affirmative action and recent ruling surrounding this practice, with students.

ASSIGNMENTS

Generating Ideas/Small-Group Discussions

ASSIGNMENT 1. After reading the "Declaration of Sentiments and Resolutions" (VI, 87), and "The Anti-Suffragists: Selected Papers, 1852–1887" (VI, 88), review Frye's "Oppression" (III, 18). Working in a small group, discuss the Seneca Falls and the Anti-Suffragist documents. List the reasons that women wanted full political participation, and list the variety of rationales offered for denying women the right to vote and participate as full citizens in the political body. What do you think about these rationales? Do they seem appropriate to their time period? Whose interest do they serve? In class discussion, compare your group's observations with those of other groups.

ASSIGNMENT 2. In light of recent debates about gay marriage and domestic partnership legislation, read *Bower* v. *Hardwick* (VI, 104) and Ettelbrick's "Confronting Obstacles to Lesbian and Gay Equality" (VI, 105). Working in a small group, identify Ettelbrick's argument about civil rights protection for gays and lesbians. List each of the obstacles she identifies. In class discussion, try to come to consensus on the future of full legal equality for gays and lesbians. Is Ettelbrick optimistic or pessimistic? Use evidence from the essay to support your view.

ASSIGNMENT 3. Working in a pair, compare the language used to describe black Americans in *Dred Scott* v. *Sandford* (VI, 90) with the language identified by the U.S. Commission on Human Rights as used to describe Native Americans in "Indian Tribes: A Continuing Quest for Survival" (VI, 83). Now look at the language used to describe women in *Bradwell* v. *Illinois* (VI, 94). What similarities can you identify in the attitudes held toward these groups of people? What effect did these attitudes have? How have these attitudes shaped history? In class discussion, compare your pair's observations with those of other pairs.

ASSIGNMENT 4. Read "The Black Codes" (VI, 93). Du Bois provides an account of the systemic attempts to deprive black Americans of their full and fair social and economic livelihood. In your journal, reflect on what the Black Codes mean for American history. Is this a different view of American history from what you have been taught thus far? What do the Black Codes reveal about whites?

Writing Assignments

ASSIGNMENT 5. The Seneca Falls Convention drafted the "Declaration of Sentiments and Resolutions" (VI, 87), purposely modeled on the Declaration of Independence. Write an essay comparing the two documents. What was the strategic purpose of modeling the one document on the other? Was this effective, do you think? Why or why not?

ASSIGNMENT 6. Read *Korematsu* v. *United States,* 1944 (VI, 100) closely, especially the introductory section on the historical and political context of the document. The Supreme Court defended the military's practice of wartime incarceration of Japanese Americans on the basis of national security, claiming that it was not an instance of racial discrimination and that "To cast this case into outlines of racial prejudice . . . merely confuses the issue." Assess the court's claim. Remember to keep in mind other readings in the collection, such as those of Omi and Winant (I, 1), Sethi (II, 14), and

Kochiyama (V, 60). You might also look up the text of the recently passed Patriot Act and think about what that text codifies with regard to issues of national security and civil liberties.

ASSIGNMENT 7. Read *People* v. *Hall, Elk* v. *Wilkins,* and *Korematsu* v. *United States* (VI, 88, 96, 99). What notion of nationalism emerges from these cases? Write an essay on American nationalism in which you consider *who* is an "American." On the basis of court cases such as these, consider the differences between the material and the ideal notion of America. Rely on writers such as Brodkin (I, 4) and Kochiyama (V, 59) to confirm or complicate your observations.

Research/Analysis Projects

ASSIGNMENT 8. *Brown* v. *Board of Education of Topeka,* 1954 (VI, 100) is a landmark case, but this court victory was long fought for and hardly the triumph of justice that we like to imagine. Few realize that *Brown* was preceded by many school desegregation cases. The *Brown* decision should be remembered in terms of the long education struggle—lasting more than 100 years—that preceded it, and the subsequent failure of governments to desegregate the schools even in the present. For this project, research the history of the school desegregation court cases and the *Brown* decision. You might start by referring back to Jay Lindsay's "Study Finds the Nation's Public School Districts Are Resegregating by Race" (III, 40) for an overview. Did African Americans universally endorse *Brown*? Why or why not? How much time elapsed after *Brown* before school desegregation was enforced nationwide? What factors continue to present obstacles to equal educational facilities and opportunities? What does the history of the case and its context suggest about the role of the legal system in race relations?

ASSIGNMENT 9. Research the history of the Equal Rights Amendment. How long have women been fighting for this amendment? What is its significance? Why was it defeated? List as many factors as you can find. Do you think it would have been a worthwhile addition to the Constitution? Why or why not?

ASSIGNMENT 10. Research the history of sexual harassment. When did sexual harassment become a crime? When was it widely recognized as a problem? When did suing employers for harassment become acceptable for women? Refer to "Wal-Martyrs" by Meg Cox (III, 26) to flesh out your discussion. You might also consider interviewing members of your family who have been in the workforce for at least 20 years. What do they remember about harassment in the workplace? Do they agree on what harassment is? Do they think that change in social recognition of the problem is a positive move?

ASSIGNMENT 11. After examining "The Anti-Suffragists: Selected Papers 1852–1887" (VI, 87), spend some time researching feminism and women's rights in the media. Listen to Rush Limbaugh or other AM talk radio, watch Fox News talk shows (especially *The O'Reilly Factor*) or Bill Maher's show on HBO, and assess how women and women's rights are covered by such sources. What are the parallels to the anti-suffragists' arguments? What are the implications of those parallels?

ASSIGNMENT 12. After reviewing "Indian Tribes: A Continuing Quest for Survival" and *Elk v. Wilkins* (VI, 436, 478), research some aspect of the history of Native American relations in the United States. You may choose to focus on more distant history—the Indian wars, the establishment of the reservation system, boarding schools, and the like—or more recent events, such as the American Indian Movement (AIM), Indian gaming, and the mascot controversies. Make sure to weave together the specific and the structural. Don't just make this a report; analyze your information as you go along. Why has the United States' relationship with indigenous people been so complicated? Did it have to be that way? Why or why not?

ASSIGNMENT 13. Research the history of affirmative action. Why was it created? Is it still necessary? Consider the implications of the recent controversy over the University of Michigan's School of Law's admission policy, wherein race is one of the categories that can help a student be admitted to the program. Given the history of race, race relations, and structural discrimination in the country, is this policy fair? Why or why not? Make sure you define your terms in your paper and provide specific examples.

RECOMMENDED MEDIA

- Show the documentary *The Spirit of Crazy Horse* (PBS Videos), which is about the conflict between the Lakota people and the FBI on the Pine Ridge reservation. The film details issues of citizenship, government mendacity and control, and a people's ability to determine their own lives and identity. What does this film illustrate about the lives of American Indians in this country? What does the film demonstrate about the definition of "American"?

- There are also several other video series on Native American tribes in the United States: *500 Nations*, *The Native Americans*, and *How the West Was Lost*. These can provide a great deal of context.

- You might consider showing all or part of the recent documentary series *Africans in America,* which is a fairly comprehensive history of slavery in the United States. Along these lines, the classic series *Eyes on the Prize* will give a pretty thorough view of the civil rights movement.

- *Daughters of the Dust,* directed by Julie Dash, tells the story of an extended African American family in the 1920s who leave their island community for the United States. The film allows you to discuss issues of history (the great migration, economic necessity, slavery, intraethnic relations) and other aspects of African American culture (such as dialect).

- Both *Chicano!* and *Viva la Causa: 500 Years of Chicano History* give overviews of Mexican Americans in U.S. history.

- In *Century of Women* (TBS documentary miniseries; six parts, 45 minutes each), several episodes provide historical context for the documents in Part VI. "Work and Family" and "Sexuality and Social Justice" describe policy decisions and historical events from suffrage and civil rights to the Equal Rights Amendment and sexual harassment. Ask students to draw connections from the film to documents they've read.

- Along these lines, *Not for Ourselves Alone: The Story of Elizabeth Cady Stanton and Susan B. Anthony* (PBS) is a recent documentary by Ken Burns on the early suffrage movement.

- You might also have students use the Internet to look up the texts of recent pieces of legislation, for example, California's anti-immigrant Proposition 187 (which has been challenged in the courts) or its Proposition 209, which effectively ended affirmative action on the state level in California. How do these propositions fit into the rest of U.S. legal history?

PART VII

Maintaining Race, Class, and Gender Hierarchies: Social Control

In addition to overt manifestations of social control, such as violence, ideologies of difference—the beliefs that uphold the claims of meaningful and inevitable differences between us—are insidious forms of social control perpetrated by the words and images we use and view every day. The challenge of Part VII lies in conveying to students the ways in which language and images construct reality: what we think and believe, and how we act. Some students will reject the idea that language and images have any power to create and maintain social inequities, because to acknowledge this is to admit to participating in systems of domination. One implication of the articles in this part is that the language we use functions to sustain illusions for the privileged, permitting a willful ignorance both of social conditions and of the part we all play every day in sustaining social hierarchies to our own advantage and sometimes to our *dis*advantage as well. It is this unintentional aspect of many of the images and words we see and use—the seemingly neutral, "what could be the harm?" attitude—that contributes to sustaining the sense that words and images are harmless. Ask students, in preparation for this part, to review Part V for personal accounts of the effects of prejudices.

ISSUES AND QUESTIONS TO CONSIDER

- Stereotypes are effective because they seem invisible; they constitute the seemingly natural. Evidence of the supposed accuracy of prejudiced beliefs is that these expectations are made manifest in the behavior of others. Paul makes us aware of the power we have over others to reproduce the evidence we may seek to justify our own cruel behavior. Ask students to discuss the role played by negative expectations in eliciting certain behaviors in others.

- Discuss the power of political language. You might define the term "hegemony" (a dominant ideology or set of controlling ideas and beliefs) and analyze how the news media perpetuates particular ways of seeing race, ethnicity, gender, sexuality, class, and ability. Refer to Macedo and Bartolome for this discussion.

- What is the role of experience in maintaining or refuting false beliefs? Can experience *always* be trusted (Paul, Mohr)?

- How do institutions such as schools, businesses, prisons, and the media maintain class divisions? Race divisions? Gender divisions? How do students internalize these lessons (Berger, Hesse-Biber, Sanday, Davis, Mantsios, Macedo and Bartolome)?

- What are the effects of making class invisible? Who benefits from social inequities? Who *really* benefits from blaming the victim? In whose interests do such strategies work (Berger, Hesse-Biber, Mantsios, Ryan)? Ask students to review Mantsios's essay in Part II as well.

- How is whiteness rendered invisible in American culture? How is blackness used to highlight or offset whiteness? How are images of people of color used to foster fantasies of white supremacy in the media (Paul, Berger, Macedo and Bartolome)?

- Cultural ideals, such as standards of beauty, seem to have no relationship to questions of social power, but how do the rewards for thinness interfere with other kinds of social rewards women might aspire to? What does this connection suggest about the relationship between gender ideals and social and economic power (Hesse-Biber)? Ask students to also refer back to Gerhart's essay in Part V.

- Violence and the threat of violence reinforce ideologies of difference by threatening those who might challenge the status quo. Ask students to name other forms of violence, such as sexual harassment, that function to keep people "in their place" (Mohr, Hesse-Biber, Chafe, Sanday).

- Ask students to consider the usefulness of art—fiction, poetry, painting, performance, music, and so on—in identifying and describing social problems. Refer to the ways Chafe uses novels to illustrate his points. What is the role of art? Especially consider this question in light of how much image making is in the service of creating and maintaining social hierarchies in popular culture (Berger, Hesse-Biber, Mantsios, Macedo and Bartolome).

- Ask students to review Paul's analysis of the psychology of bias in conjunction with Hesse-Biber's discussion of feminine beauty. How does self-hatred become internalized? How does internalizing such ideals reinforce them? What are the risks to women who refuse to conform to feminine ideals? What strategies can women adopt to work against these images?

- How does Angela Davis make visible the structural inequalities inherent in the prison system in the United States? What points does she make? How do students respond to those points? Should we worry about how this country treats its prisoners? Why or why not?

ASSIGNMENTS

Generating Ideas/Small-Group Discussions

ASSIGNMENT 1. Spend a week doing an "ideology hunt" in the mass media. You may choose whatever sources you want: newspapers, magazines, TV shows, films, and so on. Collect clippings or write brief summaries of your observations; at the end of the week, in your journal, assess what you came up with. How many stereotypes did you encounter? How many times was whiteness depicted as the "norm"? How often was class erased or a middle-class point of view taken for granted? And so on. You might want to limit your search to just *one* particular ideological perspective to make this more manageable. Share your discoveries with the class when you're finished.

ASSIGNMENT 2. Ryan argues that "blaming the victim" (VII, 113) is a "warfare" strategy that begins from good intentions. The appeal of this ideology for the middle class is that it protects class interests while providing a rationale compatible with their morality. Thus, in Ryan's analysis, even well-intentioned people are part of the problem. In a two-page homework assignment, discuss his analysis. How does sympathy, in certain forms, contribute to maintaining social inequities? For help in answering this question, you might refer to Tim Wise's "School Shooting and White Denial" (V, 73), in which he discusses the blindness with which suburban whites greet the mounting evidence of the causes of school shootings. Can you think of additional examples of solutions that fall under Ryan's critique? Which solutions to social problems would Ryan approve of? Which ones does he reject and why?

ASSIGNMENT 4. Paul argues that stereotyping "others" is deeply rooted and resistant to change even in the face of challenging evidence. In fact, she asserts, "We all use stereotypes, all the time, without knowing it. We have

met the enemy of equality, and the enemy is us" (VII, 105). In your journal, write down examples of gender, race, or class bias you suspect you
engage in unconsciously. Analyze your own reaction times in situations
where you deal with someone who is different than you. Does being conscious of your own thought processes help or hurt your ability to challenge? Discuss your own attempts at "de-automization," as Paul puts it.

ASSIGNMENT 5. Several of the essays in Part VII proceed from the identification and analysis of cultural narratives, which are the stories or rationales people tell themselves to suggest that the social order is inevitable or,
at least, that it makes sense. Some examples are: "Boys are more rational
than girls," "Women need a man to take care of them," "There will always
be poor people because it's their fault they're poor," "Blacks are lazy,"
"Chicanos have too many children," "Asians are meek and hard workers,"
"The Irish are heavy drinkers," "Gays are mentally ill," "Disabled people
are incapable of doing complex tasks." Keep a journal entry for one week
in which you write down every cultural narrative you hear someone use to
explain away a social condition or someone's behavior. Be sure to note the
circumstance in which you heard it, and jot down any that you're uncer-
tain of. At the end of the week, as a class, compile everyone's findings.
What kinds of circumstances were explained by prejudiced or mistaken
beliefs? How frequently were such rationales invoked? What do the narratives you heard say about your social environments?

Writing Assignments

ASSIGNMENT 6. Paul discusses research that identifies how bias operates
at an unconscious level even among the seemingly most unprejudiced people (VII, 105). Mohr describes the failure of empirical studies to dislodge
stereotypes that have a "social function" (VII, 106). Both Paul and Mohr
suggest the limits of education and research to change people's minds about
deeply rooted views. Yet, clearly, as Mohr puts it, a "willful ignorance of
society's workings" greatly contributes to the perpetuation of false beliefs.
These two writers believe in the importance of continued research and education to effect change. Write an essay in which you consider the value of
education as a transformative enterprise.

ASSIGNMENT 7. Compare the theories of Miller (I, 11) and Chafe (VII,
110) on how sexism and racism are maintained in U.S. society. Start by identifying the arguments each writer makes. Chafe claims that the analogy of sex
and race is a useful explanatory model for oppression because, despite their
differences, both women and people of color endure the condition that "others have controlled the power to define one's existence." Similarly, Miller dis-

cusses our tendency to internalize beliefs and behaviors that mirror social expectations of us, even when such behavior is not in our best interest. Compare in detail the arguments made by each writer. Where do the writers differ in emphasis? Are their views compatible? How useful are these theories in explaining the ways that social hierarchies are maintained?

ASSIGNMENT 8. After reading Mantsios's "Media Magic" (VII, 111) write an essay in which you discuss what else you think the media renders invisible besides or in addition to class. You could refer to Maurice Berger's piece "White Lies" (VII, 107) if you want to bring in a discussion of how whiteness, unless we look at it carefully, is also made invisible in the media. At any rate, choose some aspect of our lives and discuss how the media frames it. What is made visible? What are you not encouraged to see? What is the effect of all of this?

Research/Analysis Projects

ASSIGNMENT 9. Read Ryan's "Blaming the Victim" (VII, 113), and pay particular attention to his example of lead paint posters. Find an example of a public service announcement currently being broadcast in your local or regional news. Research the issue the poster or ad addresses. Analyze the ad to determine who is being blamed. Who does the ad address? What type of solution does the ad advocate? Does your example bear out Ryan's argument?

ASSIGNMENT 10. In his article, Ryan discusses a little bit of the history of social Darwinism. What is this? What is its history? Write a paper in which you first research the history of this particular ideology and then discuss whether or not you think it's a thing of the past. Go back and survey some of the documents in Part VI from the nineteenth century and see if this ideology is manifested there. If you don't think social Darwinism is a thing of the past, how is it currently manifested? What beliefs or messages in American culture today manifest a social Darwinist ideology? A place to start on this project might be to survey current business practices and beliefs. What is the mantra for the proper way to run a business or corporation? What do business journals or magazines say about competition? Or you might consider the slew of reality shows on TV. What is the premise of shows as seemingly disparate as *Survivor, The Bachelorette, Blind Date,* and *Fear Factor*? Why are people so captivated by them?

ASSIGNMENT 11. Sanday's "Pulling Train" (VII, 109) illustrates the role of violence as a characteristic through which masculinity is defined. Select three different masculine icons from popular culture (e.g., one of the

James Bonds, Sylvester Stallone, Nicholas Cage, Arnold Schwarzenegger, Jean-Claude van Damme, Keanu Reeves, Tom Cruise, Ben Affleck, Wesley Snipes, Bruce Willis, Harrison Ford, Will Smith, Jackie Chan). Compare the visions of the masculine ideal that they portray. Is violence a crucial dimension of their masculine identity? What kind of violent acts do they engage in? What other attributes can you identify by which we know they are *men*? Kimmel's "Masculinity as Homophobia" (I, 8) will also be helpful here.

ASSIGNMENT 12. Read Hesse-Biber (VII, 108) and review Lorber (I, 5), Hubbard (I, 6), and Gerhart (V, 76). Also look back over the essays discussing masculinity and men. Then either watch commercials surrounding a "woman's show" (soap operas, *Oprah Winfrey,* a women's sporting event, etc.) and a "man's show" (sports, news, an action show, etc.) or compile a selection of ads from women's and men's magazines for similar product lines. Compare the ways marketers target women and men. What did you find? How do advertisers construct gender differently in the commercials or ads? What assumptions do the ads seem to make about male and female consumers? How do those assumptions influence the ways women and men act? Feel? Think of themselves? Why do you think capitalism promotes gender differences in advertising? How does capitalism directly benefit from gender differences?

ASSIGNMENT 13. Read Mantsios's "Media Magic: Making Class Invisible" (VII, 111). Tape or just watch and take notes of the local evening TV news on one station for a week. Either make an edited tape of news stories or summarize the stories you saw that illustrate Mantsios's points about the construction of class divisions. Study the stories in terms of the class narratives they offer. How are white-collar professionals depicted? How are the rural poor depicted? The urban poor? Can you identify patterns in the ways certain groups are depicted in your town or region? Are Mantsios's observations applicable? How? Did you see different narratives? What were they? Write an essay on your findings, and do a presentation on it in class.

ASSIGNMENT 14. After reading Davis's "Masked Racism: Reflections on the Prison Industrial Complex" (VII, 112), research the history of the prison system in the United States and how it compares to that of other industrialized nations around the world. What does Davis mean by "masked racism"? How does she define the "prison industrial complex" in her essay? Why are so many people incarcerated in the United States today? How does that compare to incarceration rates in the past? What is the difference between an ideology of reform and an ideology of punishment? What do you think works best? Why? Write a paper that fully explores these questions as you consider the history of incarceration in the United States. Make sure you connect your discussion up with other concepts covered in the book so far.

RECOMMENDED MEDIA

- Science-fiction films can offer a great deal of insight into the ways society organizes itself. For a simple, useful, and fun—albeit a bit crude—portrayal of how ideology works, show John Carpenter's cult classic *They Live.* Ask students to focus on the moment when the main character finally "sees" the ideological underpinnings of what he has previously taken for granted. Also ask students to think about what the aliens represent in the film. For a more current take on this issue, you might also show *Matrix* and its sequels.

- You might also directly address the power of blockbuster films to help create and maintain hierarchies. Compare and contrast how race and gender are dealt with in *Independence Day,* where the white, male, middle-aged president of the United States is the one to do the final elimination of the alien invaders (Will Smith's fighter pilot notwithstanding), and a film like *Anaconda*, where one white male is disabled for almost the entire film and another is eventually eaten by a giant snake, leaving a young Latina (Jennifer Lopez) and a young African American man (Ice Cube) to save the day. These are perfect films to analyze in this context because they are not "arty" or "political" but rather as students always love to point out, "just entertainment."

- Show one of the recent crop of "women's films" such as *Maid in New York* or *How to Lose a Guy in Ten Days.* Ask students to analyze the film for its construction of femininity, masculinity, heterosexuality, gender relations, class, and race. What stories do these films tell women? What are the consequences of those stories? But also, why are they powerful? What hopes do they fill women, in particular, with?

- *Slim Hopes* or *Killing Us Softly III,* both directed by Jean Kilbourne, trace the media's use of women's bodies to sell products and examine the ways in which women's bodies simultaneously become objectified, commodified, and infantilized. In the former film, Kilbourne addresses the issue of eating disorders as a result of such depictions. You might also consider showing Walt Disney's *Cinderella* in order to look at how even as children, girls are socialized to be pretty, masochistic, and competitive. If girls are meant to aspire to be Cinderellas, where does that leave them?

- Spike Lee's *Bamboozled*, together with the documentary, *Ethnic Notions,* interrogate the long-standing stereotypical depictions of African Americans in popular culture. Lee's film, a biting satire of the film and television industry, takes as its premise the creation of a nouveau minstrel show by an ambitious African American comedy writer. Pairing this often painful, often funny film with *Ethnic Notions,* which is referenced in *Bamboozled,* is a great way to introduce students to the long legacy of racist imagery in popular culture.

- Along these lines, you could also show *Color Adjustment,* directed by Marlon Riggs, which portrays the history of the representation of black Americans on network TV in the United States and insistently poses the questions: What counts as a *positive* social image, and what counts as *negative*? Ask students to consider changes in the representation of black Americans since Riggs's film was made. You might also show a clip from *Birth of a Nation* to establish some of the historical context of media and societal representations of African American people.

- You might check out the website for the Media Education Foundation website (www.mediaed.org). Videos such as *The Myth of the Liberal Media,* which is a very useful outline and explication of Noam Chomsky's propaganda model of the media, and Sut Jhally's *Advertising and the End of the World,* which details the pervasive ideological aspects of the advertising industry and its implication in major environmental disasters, are produced by this nonprofit organization. Jean Kilbourne's videos are offered here, as are videotaped interviews with bell hooks, Edward Said, and Stuart Hall.

PART VIII

Making a Difference: Social Activism

By the time you come to the end of *Race, Class and Gender in the United States,* students might feel somewhat disheartened at the state of things in the United States. Although many of the essays throughout the text offer solutions to the problems they name, students often come away with the sense that the articles have been primarily concerned with describing the inequities many Americans face. Part VIII is designed to address these issues by giving readers concrete strategies for enacting social change. The essays here enable readers to re-envision the future, to "make a difference" in the world, and to offer alternative narratives for how our society can (and should) be. New to the sixth edition, in particular, are several essays and articles that focus on student activism. You may want to ask students to consider the generic distinctions between these selections and those in other parts. Also, you may want to have students review selections from Part I in particular to remind them of the economic basis for race, gender, sexuality, and class constructions.

The assignments in this part are designed to focus students' attention on the details of the arguments presented here to help them acquire a critical vocabulary to use beyond the classroom. Focusing their attention on the details of the arguments has another benefit as well: only when students truly understand what they object to should they launch their own critique. This view does not seek to shut down students' voices; rather, it insists that students have logical, reasoned responses to the arguments with which they disagree. You may want to remind them that even when they disagree with an argument, they may still learn quite a lot from it. Then, if inspired, students will be able to begin their own activist projects or at least continue the difficult task of constructing their own critical lenses of the world in which they live.

ISSUES AND QUESTIONS TO CONSIDER

- Ask students what the value is of trying to change oppressive social systems. You might spend some time defining the term "utopia" (a good basic definition is "the no place which is the good place," which draws on the Greek origin of the word) and tying it to the work of the authors in this part. Is "utopian thinking" hopelessly passé and ridiculously naïve? Or is it a necessary impulse that sparks social change? Utopias have traditionally functioned as critiques of the author's own society. You might point that out to students as well.

- What does it mean to "rethink differences"? Ask students to consider why none of the positions set forth in Part VIII suggest disregarding differences. You might refer back to the question concerning "color blindness" and "gender neutrality" in the "Issues and Questions to Consider" section of Part III in this manual. In whose interest is it to overlook differences?

- Blanchard takes issue with the school of thought that focuses on economic disparities as being more oppressive than racism. What do students make of his argument? What must "white folks" do to end racism?

- How does the "ally" model "interrupt the cycle of oppression"? Ask students to assess Ayvazian's use of this term and its effectiveness.

- Do the writers in this part argue for social change or social transformation? What is the difference between the two concepts? What are the conditions the writers identify as requiring transformation? What are the conditions they suggest that would make transformation possible? How have people engaged in transformative projects? You might spend some time with your students assessing the goals of the various activist projects Part VIII includes.

- Attentiveness to the structure and detail of everyday life has been a constant thread throughout this volume, urging us to focus on the tangible and immediate rather than the abstract and transcendent. How does Bronski use the simple gesture of holding his lover's hand on the way to the movies to make his point? Why does he relate this to his readers? How do the articles about student activists force your students to think about the t-shirts they might be wearing or the tacos they eat? How do other authors use the category of the everyday and to what effect?

- These articles emphasize the need for the redistribution of power if any kind of meaningful social change is to be effected. Some students will find this liberating but many will find it threatening, even those who might stand to gain the most from such change. Ask students to focus their attention on why *these* solutions are the ones selected for the volume. What does the magnitude of the proposed solutions suggest about the severity of the problems described (Ayvazian, Dalton, Blanchard, Bronski, Hout and Lucas)?

- Ask students to consider how their lives would be different if fundamental social change were to occur. Would their lives improve or decline? What is their investment in maintaining things just as they are?

- Ask students if they have ever cared deeply enough about an issue to do something tangible about it. Are they members of any sort of activist groups? Why or why not?

ASSIGNMENTS

Generating Ideas/Small-Group Discussions

ASSIGNMENT 1. Your instructor will bring a selection of pens, pencils, and some poster boards or large pieces of paper to class. Get into a group of four to five people. The group's task will be to draw a map of a utopia. Many people believe that a utopia is an ideal world. Others try to make a literal blueprint of a utopia—with varying results. An interesting idea to start from for this assignment is the notion that a utopia is "the no place which is the good place." In other words, it's a place that does not literally exist except in the ideal; it's an impulse, something to work *toward*. For this assignment, then, the group members can draw a literal map or draw a representation of their utopia. They should spend time negotiating what they want their utopia to be (which may be difficult since people may want different things). Make sure your group considers such issues as race, class, gender, and sexuality systems; economics; education; the environment; government; and resources. How will the group's utopia deal with all of these things? How will this new world be different from the one we live in now? When the map is finished, group members should spend some time summarizing their utopia to present it to the rest of the class. After every group has presented its utopia, review the definition stated above. How does conceptualizing a different world help you think about the one we live in now? How does that impulse to conceive of "the good place" make you try to do something concrete here? Does it make you want to do something here? Or does the gap between the actual and the ideal seem too large for you? How can a project like this open up your mind to think about things in new and different ways? Is there value in that?

ASSIGNMENT 2. In groups, identify a social issue that you want to do something about. You might review Sklar's "Imagine a Country—2003" (IV, 47) for ideas to help you with this assignment. Be specific and focused. Map out a strategy for doing something about your issue. Use the students against sweatshops, the protests against Taco Bell, and the SEIU articles as guides. When you're finished, reconvene with the rest of the class and present your plan.

ASSIGNMENT 3. Read the essay by Bronski (VIII, 118) and "Rice Shirts Make More Than Fashion Statement" (VIII, 119). Both pieces focus on the prevalence of homophobia in our society and how such attitudes threaten the freedom of gay people to function comfortably in U.S. society. Spend some time in your journal outlining each author's solution to combating homophobia. How do the pieces complement each other?

ASSIGNMENT 4. Read "Child of the Americas" by Aurora Levins Morales (VIII, 126). In your journal, consider the role that creativity can play in imagining transformative solutions. What can poetry convey that prose cannot? What can prose provide that poetry cannot? How does the poem work with the prose selections? In general, what can art offer to social activism?

Writing Assignments

ASSIGNMENT 5. What student movements are happening on your campus? What do you think of them? Are you participating in any of them? How? Do you plan on joining one or more? Why or why not? Write a short essay in which you consider these questions. What does activism mean to you? What do you think it can do? Be sure to include specific examples with your assessment of these groups' efficacy.

ASSIGNMENT 6. Read "Interrupting the Cycle of Oppression: The Role of Allies as Agents of Change" by Andrea Ayvazian (VIII, 116). What is an "ally"? Does Ayvazian's use of the term provide an adequate model for people in dominant positions in the culture or people with relative power to enact social change? How? Write an essay in which you discuss Ayvazian's article and the term "ally." Make sure you provide some concrete examples in your paper.

ASSIGNMENT 7. According to Fletcher Blanchard (VIII, 622), what must whites do to help end racism and bigotry? Write an essay in which you consider Blanchard's analysis of overt racism and unintentional, well-meaning bigotry. What do you think of this essay? What did you learn from it? In your estimation, will the author's solutions work? Why or why not?

ASSIGNMENT 8. Review Morales's poem "Child of the Americas" (VIII, 126). Write your own poem or short prose piece in which you describe the circumstances that compel someone to acknowledge the world's pain, the kind of heroic figure who manifests change, or some future world in which transformation can occur.

ASSIGNMENT 9. Select any one essay or article from Part VIII. Write a summary of the argument and an explanation of the views presented. Be sure to pay careful attention to the specific positions the author holds. Use as much detail as possible to delineate the pains, challenges, and responsibilities emphasized in the essay. Focus on making the author's views clear to someone who has never read the essay.

Research/Analysis Projects

ASSIGNMENT 10. "Difference" is the basis for "identity politics," which emerged as a response to—and a rejection of—the integrationist politics of the 1960s, exemplified in the civil rights movement. Research the short history of identity politics. Why did it emerge? What are the arguments in favor of assimilation politics? What are the arguments for rejecting assimilation politics? Blanchard (VIII, 117) or Ayvazian (VIII, 116) might help you get started.

ASSIGNMENT 11. In her article, Ayvazian (VIII, 116) mentions an exercise she does with groups she is speaking to in which she asks people to name some famous racists (which always gets a big response) and then asks them to name some famous *anti*racists (which is largely met with silence). Taking Ayvazian's lead, write a research paper in which you discuss antiracism as a political practice and cite some people who have done work in this area. Some areas to look up: the abolition movement, the civil rights movement, the Black Power movement, the United Farm Workers struggles, the Chicano rights movement, and the American Indian Movement. What can you learn from doing this research? What has been the role of allies in social movements? You could also do this paper from a gender, sexuality, or class perspective as well.

ASSIGNMENT 12. In "Combating Intentional Bigotry and Inadvertently Racist Acts," Fletcher Blanchard (VIII, 117) describes an experiment he and his colleagues conducted in 1991 where they briefly interviewed students about racism as the students walked between classes. They would plant someone also walking by who would give programmed responses either expressing antiracist views or condoning racism. The subject of the experiment would then often follow suit, which led Blanchard to the conclusion that people need to take strong public stands against racism and bigotry to help end them. Working with others in a group project, look up the original article in *Psychological Science* and reenact the experiment at your school. Write up the group's findings in a collaborative paper. Did the results mirror Blanchard's or not? In what ways were your results the same or different? What are the group members' conclusions about Blanchard's solution to help end racism? Would it work? How?

ASSIGNMENT 13. In "Narrowing the Income Gap between Rich and Poor," Michael Hout and Samuel Lucas (VIII, 123) argue that wealth needs to be redistributed so that the huge gap between the rich and the poor is eliminated. To do this, they believe that a reinvigorated labor movement is key; unions "help lower the inequality of income because they typically make management more accountable to workers." After carefully reading Hout and Lucas's article, write a paper in which you research some aspect of the history of the labor movement in the United States. Pay particular attention to what the ability to unionize has done for workers. You should look at "A Clean Sweep: The SEIU's Organizing Drive for Janitors Shows How Unionization Can Raise Wages" by Harold Meyerson (VIII, 124) for an important example. Why have people fought to the point of dying for the right to organize? Try to challenge your own assumptions about labor activism and unions in this paper. In whose interest has it been to paint labor activism as extremist and dangerous? Dangerous to whom? What are the implications of a unionized labor force? Refer back to Hout and Lucas, Meyerson, and Calputura (VIII, 125) to help you with your conclusion.

ASSIGNMENT 14. Read "Sweats and Tears: A Protest Is Sweeping U.S. Campuses to End the Use of Sweatshops to Produce College-Endorsed Clothes" by Simon Birch (VIII, 120) and "United Students Against Sweatshops" (VIII, 121). Research the history of this group and write an essay about contemporary student movements. Make sure to take into account students' increasing interest in issues of globalization and international politics. Is there a chapter of SAS on your campus? Should students consider their place in the move towards globalization? What *is* globalization?

ASSIGNMENT 15. Many students may feel challenged by the material in this text. This assignment is designed to give you a constructive way to channel your energies into a project. For this service-learning project, pick an organization, group, nonprofit agency, or the like, and volunteer your time. Choose something that you feel passionate about and that has come out of the work you have done in this class. You might volunteer at a battered women's shelter or at a labor union. You could sign up to be a mentor, or teach an adult to read, or participate in a Meals-on-Wheels program. Whatever you decide to do, take notes on your experience. At the end of the class, write a paper in which you establish what your goals were, as influenced by the readings you've done in the book; what you accomplished in your position; and what you wish to do in this vein in the future. In the face of the large-scale problems we have been studying, this may seem like a small step. However, change occurs in the everyday, small actions one person does, as well as on the large-scale level.

ASSIGNMENT 16. Review newspaper articles and other materials on the antiwar movement, both domestic and international, which grew up in response to the 2003 war in Iraq. How was this movement organized? What was significant about it? What happened to it? How did the mass media frame it? Use this movement as a recent case study for how social movements form, how they work, and what they do to enact social change. Make sure your essay introduces the context for the movement, as well as describes and analyzes the movement itself.

ASSIGNMENT 17. Do a research project on a social movement in the past. You might look over the documents in Part VI and think about the movements that helped usher in legislative reforms or the movements that formed to react against what some would see as legislative setbacks. You could also read through Howard Zinn's *A People's History of the United States* to find a movement that appeals to you. Some questions you should ask yourself as you write this paper: What was the movement meant to do? Was it successful? Why or why not? Make sure you cite specific examples and that you detail what the movement achieved.

RECOMMENDED MEDIA

- If you want to do a unit on utopia/dystopia, you might begin by showing a film like *Blade Runner,* which is a dark vision of a future Los Angeles riven by racial, ethnic, extraterrestrial, and class divisions. Follow this by showing *Tank Girl,* where the title character of this story (based on a comic book by the same name) is a savvy counterculture guerrilla fighter who is the heroine of a future California run by a corporation that hoards natural resources. This film raises questions about power, mixed identity, and sexuality in a funky, funny setting. *Alien II* is another science-fiction thriller about a strong woman who battles both the evil corporate empire and a strange new threat from deep space. Along with these films, you might also consider assigning a novel or two. Octavia E. Butler's 20-minutes-into-the-future take on a dystopian Los Angeles, *Parable of the Sower,* also contains seeds of utopian renewal via community, cooperation, and spirituality. Charlotte Perkins Gilman's 1890s feminist utopia, *Herland,* is interesting to pair with Butler's text because while it contests dominant gender and class roles, it is terrible on race and ethnicity and silent on sexuality. As you go through this section, ask students to consider why the science-fiction genre is so often chosen to portray future change. Also, what do these texts do with gender? Race and ethnicity? Class? Sexuality?

- Part VIII also works well when it is paired with depictions of activism. Try showing the documentary *Berkeley in the Sixties* and discuss student activism from the free speech movement to the antiwar movement. You can go even farther back and show a film like *The Grapes of Wrath* and discuss how it entered into discussions of what to do for poor people during the Great Depression. You can then link this film to other media forms, such as the songs of Woody Guthrie, Bob Dylan, Joan Baez, and Pete Seeger on through to contemporary artist-activists like Ani DiFranco and Bruce Springsteen (whose album *The Ghost of Tom Joad* references both *The Grapes of Wrath* and Guthrie's work). *Eyes on the Prize* or any of the filmed speeches of Dr. Martin Luther King, Jr., speak to efforts to end racism. All of these texts offer students concrete representations of how people have organized to contest the oppressive structures in which they live.

- For a contemporary and quite funny representation of guerrilla activism, rent a tape of some episodes of Michael Moore's *The Awful Truth.* Consult Moore's website to find out how to get copies of his work. Students will respond to Moore's lively engagement with corporate and public figures and his unwillingness to allow the status quo to go unchallenged. Ask students whether or not they think this kind of activism is effective and why.

- Show *Norma Rae* and discuss Norma's transformation from an oppressed factory worker to an empowered union organizer. How do Norma and her coworkers benefit materially from her efforts? How is Norma oppressed by her class and gender before her transformation? How does the film deal with race?

- Similarly, show *Salt of the Earth* and discuss how the characters in the film are transformed through their labor activism.

- Ken Loach's film, *Bread and Roses,* is a wonderful fictional depiction of the janitors' struggle to unionize in downtown Los Angeles. This would be a wonderful pairing with Meyerson's and Calputura's articles on the same topic.